MAKING THE
CURRICULUM WORK

for Learners with Dyslexia

Jenny Lee

Acknowledgements

For ideas and suggestions for this book, grateful thanks to:

Clive Blueman, Pat Evans, Kristin Hutchinson and Lesley Turner, LEAP Adult Education Centre, Durham LEA

Ray Lee, University of Sheffield, Dyslexia Research Unit

Chris Murray, Newcastle City Council Adult Basic Education Service

Lauraine Parkinson, Handsworth College of Further Education

Jean Walker and Staff at The Dyslexic Institute, Sheffield.

Note:

As the dyslexic male/female ratio is about 3:1 and the basic skills teacher female/male ratio is much higher, for the purpose of ease of reading, I will refer throughout this book to the learner as 'he' and the tutor as 'she', although clearly this is by no means always the case.

Published November 2002

ISBN 1 85990 214 6

Design: Studio 21

Contents

1 Introduction

'I'm trying, God knows I'm trying. Can you not help?'

THIS extract from a piece of writing by Clive, a dyslexic learner, eloquently describes the frustration he felt when being taught by a teacher who did not understand the special teaching methods needed for a person with dyslexia to learn successfully.

He continues:

'Inside I'm crying. Can you not feel?
Hope is dying, doors slam shut'.

Blame, if blame there be, is neither with him nor with his teacher. He or she, if not dyslexia trained would have been equally baffled when perfectly good tried and tested teaching methods just would not work with this particular student.

Reliable research suggests that between 4% and 10% of the population is dyslexic (Badian, 1984 and Pennington, 1991). This percentage will obviously increase in a basic skills setting. In our LEA basic skills centre in County Durham, we have a specialist adult dyslexia unit where teachers who have undertaken specialist training, work with dyslexic learners, often on a one to one basis or in small groups. In our centre we estimate that around 20% of learners are dyslexic and this sizeable minority will not learn effectively using normal teaching methods.

The main purpose of this handbook is to enable both tutors and dyslexic learners to appreciate the opportunities the new *Adult Literacy and Numeracy Core Curriculum* can offer and how it can be made to work for these learners. The Curriculum's structured framework, focusing as it does on text, sentence and word levels, is a valuable starting point from which to develop a structured multisensory programme tailored to the individual dyslexic learner's needs.

An understanding of the nature of dyslexia is important as the basic skills teacher must be able to explain to the learner why these specialist methods should be adhered to. Therefore some information on current research into the subject will be given.

Some suggestions for teaching approaches will be offered, but the list is by no means exhaustive nor, regrettably, will all methods work for everyone. Thus another purpose of this handbook is to open up a forum for debate and dissemination of good practice in the teaching of dyslexic adults.

> 'The quality of current provision (for adults with dyslexia) is perceived as being uneven and inadequate . . . Very few basic skills courses are appropriate for dyslexic students. Basic skills tutors and managers lack knowledge about dyslexia. In particular there is a lack of awareness of the role language processing plays in literacy acquisition'
>
> (*Freedom to Learn*, DfEE, 2000)

We welcome correspondence, advice, suggestions, even criticism! This book should not be seen as a definitive guide but rather as a catalyst to initiate the debate.

'If they don't learn the way we teach,
we must teach the way they learn.'

(Traditional)

IF Clive's teacher could have discovered what particular way that was, much of the frustration both he and his teacher experienced could have been avoided.

The Keys to Dyslexia Teaching and Learning

There are 5 keys to successful dyslexia teaching.

1. Learning must be multisensory.
2. There must be an enormous amount of overlearning.
3. Learning must be structured and carefully paced.
4. Phonological awareness may need to be taught to some learners during the early stages.
5. The tutor and the learner must both be involved in learning about learning (metacognition). In other words, both tutor and learner must understand why the first four keys are so important, as well as experimenting with strategies to discover the learner's own best learning styles.

Some Relevant Theory

Don't switch off here, this bit is interesting!

Most dyslexia researchers now agree that dyslexia is caused by physical and hence physiological differences in the brain which result in the dyslexic individual having problems in processing language.

There are 3 main regions of the brain which have been identified in dyslexia research; the language areas, the cerebellum and the magnocellular regions which deal with temporal processing.

1. The Language Areas

a) Multisensory Learning

Paulesu and Frith (1996) studied the language area in the left hemisphere of the brain and found that there is a bridge (the Insula) between the part of the brain that processes what we hear (Broca's Area) and the part that processes what we see (Wernicke's Area). When this bridge is working normally, we can translate automatically what we **see** into an internal speech code (we say it in our heads) and what we **hear** into a mental picture. In other words, we use multisensory strategies quite naturally.

In research with dyslexic adults, this bridge has been found to be working inefficiently. It seems that they do not automatically translate from an auditory code to visual or vice versa. Therefore unlike non dyslexic people they can only use one modality when learning rather than two. Because of this, learning to read or spell will be slower and less efficient.

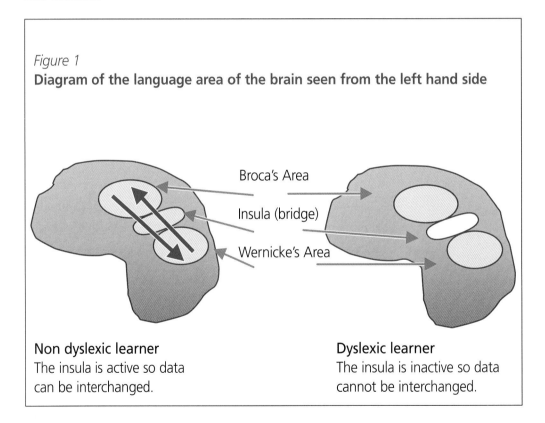

Figure 1
Diagram of the language area of the brain seen from the left hand side

Broca's Area

Insula (bridge)

Wernicke's Area

Non dyslexic learner
The insula is active so data
can be interchanged.

Dyslexic learner
The insula is inactive so data
cannot be interchanged.

It seems unlikely (but we do not know) that this broken bridge could be mended, but what we can do in multisensory teaching is to activate the two areas at the same time so that the student simultaneously sees and hears whatever it is he wants to learn.

Using a diagram such as the one opposite to explain the reasoning behind some of the strange things we ask dyslexic learners to do will help to clarify our first statement: that learning must be multisensory.

b) Working Memory

Nearly all dyslexic people have deficits in working memory[1]: that is remembering and being able to manipulate in the head what has just been heard (Rack 1994). Why should this be? One theory is that they have an initial difficulty with phonological awareness (being able to discriminate and segment sounds in words). Working memory relies on phonological awareness because when it is necessary to remember something that has just been heard or seen, like a telephone number, the standard strategy would be to repeat it over and over using an internal speech code (rehearsal). Therefore if phonological awareness is faulty, then working memory is also likely to be weak. Learning how to read and spell relies heavily on both hearing clearly all the sounds in words (phonological awareness) and remembering the sequence of these sounds (working memory).

c) Phonological Awareness

Nearly all severely dyslexic adults demonstrate difficulty when tested on their ability to identify, segment and manipulate sounds in words and sometimes to make rhyme judgements. This well documented skill of phonological awareness is crucial to the development of reading and spelling skills. Many researchers including Rack, Hulme and Snowling (for a summary see Snowling, 2001) have repeatedly demonstrated the dyslexic individual's difficulty with this. Early phonological awareness development should be a prerequisite of basic literacy teaching and should continue to run alongside the early stages of teaching reading and spelling. It seems that magically, phonological awareness enhances reading skills and reading enhances phonological awareness; one developing on the back of the other. It is easy to test for phonological awareness problems by giving phoneme deletion and substitution exercises such as those in the *Dyslexia Adult Screening Test* (Fawcett & Nicolson, 1998) or in Hatcher's *Sound Linkage* (1994). Some phonological awareness exercises summarising these ideas are provided in Appendix 2 of this book.

Clearly if a student finds it difficult to segment words into their smallest sounds or phonemes, he will have problems decoding accurately and sequentially when reading and encoding when spelling. So the fourth key to dyslexia teaching, developing phonological awareness is explained.

––––––––

1. To read further on the subject of working memory, see *Access for All* (DfES, 2002).

2. The Cerebellum

The second important piece of research that has profound implications for our teaching, is the role of the cerebellum. Initially it was thought that the cerebellum was just involved with motor control. Increasingly through the work of Akshoomoff (1992) and Leiner (1993) it appears that the cerebellum has a role to play in cognition. Perhaps the most important link is that between the neocerebellum and Broca's Area, giving the cerebellum a possible role in language control and development. It seems that there are wired loops between the cerebellum and the cortex which function in much the same way as computer circuits. Nicolson and Fawcett (1994) tested a group of dyslexic people on a wide range of tests of cerebellar function and found evidence that all showed some cerebellar impairment.

The cerebellum acts to smooth cortical data by deciding what is significant and what is insignificant to any particular motor or cognitive area of activity. It feeds back to the cortex only that information which is necessary for a good executive decision. Clearly this loop can only work effectively if the cerebellum is working efficiently. If it is faulty, when a student is reading, the executive decision might result in the wrong word being read. If the student is spelling then letter reversals or faulty phonology might be the decision.

The dyslexic individual's well documented difficulties with short term or working memory are now being associated with the cerebellum's role in articulation (a motor skill) as well as being centred in the language area. Any fault in the cerebellum or the cerebellar cortical loop seems to impair the ability to internally articulate (saying it in your head) which impacts on phonological awareness which is fundamental to efficient working memory. As stated earlier, learning to read and spell is highly dependent on good working memory skills.

Consequently, if a dyslexic adult is to succeed, attention must be paid to articulation skills. This is another reason why the regular repetitions, which occur throughout specialist multisensory programmes, are so important.

Another function of the cerebellum has been described by Fawcett and Nicolson (2001) through their work on cerebellar impairment; automaticity and conscious compensation. Normally when learning, if data is processed accurately, the person becomes automatic in the skill being practised. Once a skill is automatic any cortical activity is then strictly controlled by the cerebellum. The skill can be carried out fluently without distractions.

Nicolson and Fawcett argue that this state of automaticity is very difficult to achieve if you are dyslexic, because the faulty cerebellum will not process data of a consistent quality to allow automatisation to occur. They assess that up to 100 more learning opportunities are likely to be necessary for the skill levels to approach normality. They think this is why the dyslexic student has to work so much harder than his peers to achieve the same standard. In effect, the student is using the cortex and learning for extended periods. This means that the capacity for higher order reading skills such as comprehension is diminished in the dyslexic learner's brain because he has failed to automatise.

In simple terms, the dyslexic individual is in a virtually permanent state of learning, finding it very difficult to achieve the status of having learned or mastered a skill.

This lack of automaticity will also affect memory. Because a skill such as spelling is not automatic, memory traces are still likely to be dependent on cognitive input such as working out a spelling rule. If the dyslexic learner neglects this cognitive input on spellings which are not yet automatic, then he is likely to produce the wrong spelling when dual tasking. Until the skill is automatic, the dyslexic learner will need both cognitive and cerebellar input every time the spelling is used. Having learnt a skill to the stage that it is automatic, gives the non-dyslexic individual the privilege of being able to carry it out without interference from competing activities.

The dyslexic learner's lack of automaticity might account for their well documented difficulties with distraction. Anyone who has worked with a dyslexic learner will have

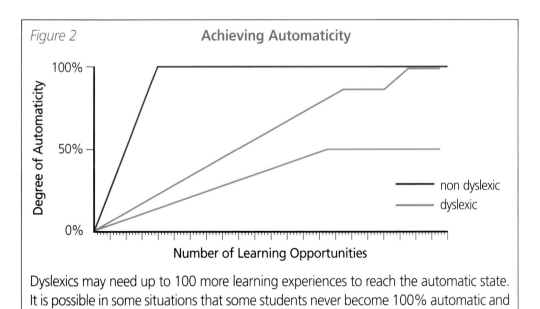

Figure 2 — Achieving Automaticity

Degree of Automaticity (y-axis: 0%, 50%, 100%)

Number of Learning Opportunities (x-axis)

non dyslexic
dyslexic

Dyslexics may need up to 100 more learning experiences to reach the automatic state. It is possible in some situations that some students never become 100% automatic and may have to re-learn constantly.

Diagram derived from Fawcett & Nicolson 1994

experienced the frustration for both tutor and learner when, despite being able to spell a word perfectly well, if he stops to think about it, the student gets it completely wrong when using it in a piece of free writing. This is because having to think about content, grammar and punctuation distracts him from the spelling.

Nicolson and Fawcett argue that dyslexic people can often achieve high standards, but only through a mechanism of conscious compensation. They recognise their difficulties and use strategies to maximise their learning. Very simply they know the extent of their task and work harder to achieve success. This is metacognition or learning about learning and knowing one's own best learning style. No wonder they are often tired and appear to switch off.

It is clear from this research why the second key to good dyslexia teaching is so important – that there must be an enormous amount of overlearning in order to take into account the dyslexic learner's difficulty in achieving automaticity.

3. Temporal and Visual Processing

The speed at which an individual processes information, both when producing language (word finding); and when receiving language (listening/understanding); is another important factor in developing phonological awareness and literacy skills. Tallal (1997) found that dyslexic people are much slower at perceiving the sounds within a syllable and differences between syllables.

It seems that many dyslexic individuals are slower at language processing than others. For instance, they will often report difficulties in keeping track of conversations when a group of people are together, or keeping up if a lecturer talks too quickly. It is therefore important, when teaching dyslexic students, to speak with plenty of pauses to give them time to process what is being said. Regular summing up of key points also helps. Giving a clear structure to any learning enables students to use their logic to enhance processing. This is the third key to dyslexic teaching.

Lovegrove (1990) and Livingstone (1991) found deficits in the visual processing systems of some dyslexic individuals. It has been shown that in some dyslexic people the magnocells (the cells in the brain that control the efficiency and speed of visual and, some think, auditory processing) are not working efficiently, although how exactly this would affect the development of reading has not yet been established. It may, however, be the cause of the visual disturbances some describe when reading continuous text, e.g. letters blurring or moving, words moving together or from line to line. Stein (2001) has also found problems in these magnocells and has found that in some cases, covering one eye when reading, varying the coloured overlay or taking a food supplement of fatty acids can help.

The importance of the fifth key, that of learning about learning should now be become clear. If the dyslexic individual is to maximise learning opportunities, it will help if he understands some of the reasons behind why he finds acquiring reading and writing skills so difficult. A greater understanding of dyslexia will reduce some of the frustration. Self esteem will increase when he appreciates that dyslexia is in no way connected with low intelligence. It helps him a great deal to understand why he needs to relearn over and over again and it is a relief to know that his tutor understands too. This understanding makes learning more of an interesting academic exercise and less of an embarrassment. He can then begin to explore his own best learning styles (he has probably been doing this subconsciously for years) and monitor, adapt and take control of his learning. This process of metacognition is the fifth key to success in dyslexic teaching and learning.

Figure 3 is a summary of the research described showing how the physical differences in the brain cause cognitive deficits which in turn impact on a person's behaviour.

It should be noted that the research described in this chapter is still being debated in scientific circles and there is a need for further work and replication. However, all the studies described seem to resonate with the experience of dyslexia practitioners.

Summary

- The keys or golden rules of dyslexia teaching that many experienced dyslexia specialists have been developing and using for years, are now becoming substantiated by scientific research.

- Structured multisensory teaching which is grounded in phonological awareness and incorporates a great deal of overlearning will, if it involves the student at all levels, result in success.

- We can now assure students that dyslexia is a real condition with physical characteristics. It is not just an excuse for bad spelling or something like Santa Claus or the tooth fairy that can be believed in or not. As one learner said after a particularly exasperating day:

'If dyslexia's 'all in the mind', then God help me!'

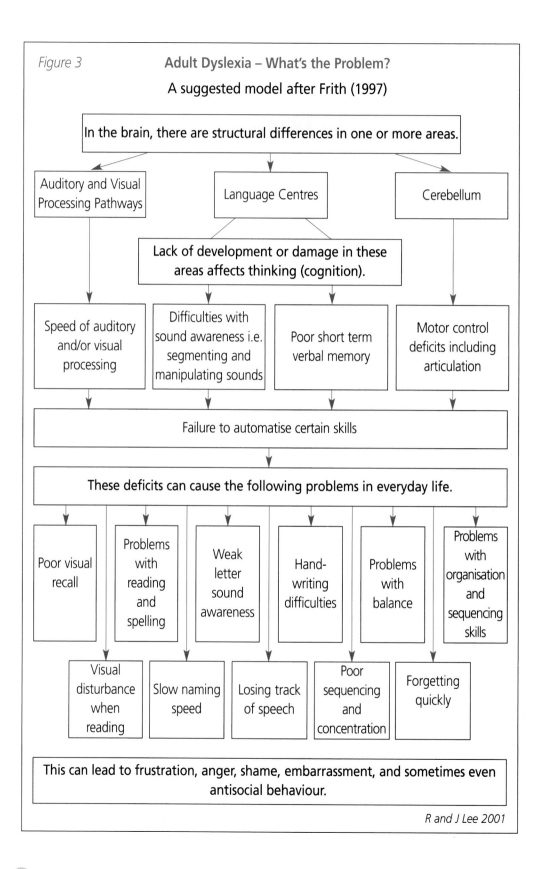

Figure 3

Adult Dyslexia – What's the Problem?

A suggested model after Frith (1997)

In the brain, there are structural differences in one or more areas.

| Auditory and Visual Processing Pathways | Language Centres | Cerebellum |

Lack of development or damage in these areas affects thinking (cognition).

| Speed of auditory and/or visual processing | Difficulties with sound awareness i.e. segmenting and manipulating sounds | Poor short term verbal memory | Motor control deficits including articulation |

Failure to automatise certain skills

These deficits can cause the following problems in everyday life.

| Poor visual recall | Problems with reading and spelling | Weak letter sound awareness | Hand-writing difficulties | Problems with balance | Problems with organisation and sequencing skills |

| Visual disturbance when reading | Slow naming speed | Losing track of speech | Poor sequencing and concentration | Forgetting quickly |

This can lead to frustration, anger, shame, embarrassment, and sometimes even antisocial behaviour.

R and J Lee 2001

3

Characteristics of dyslexia –
identifying the problems of dyslexia in the basic skills
population

'Reading is intense work'

IN the last chapter, we touched upon dyslexic people's ability to compensate for their difficulties, sometimes even without realising they are doing so. The man who made the statement at the beginning of this chapter did not appear to be having difficulty with reading, but, because of his lack of automaticity in word recognition and decoding, the task was in fact extremely onerous.

It can sometimes be difficult to identify among a group of adult basic skills dyslexic learners, the ones who are most at risk of being dyslexic. On the following pages are some of the characteristics common to most dyslexic adults (Figure 4). It should be noted, however, that many people have some of these indications, but people with dyslexia will be likely to have a number. If dyslexia seems a possibility, then expert assessment should be sought from a psychologist or specialist teacher. This checklist can be photocopied and used with learners.

If a learner seems to have a number of the characteristics described in this checklist, a good screening test which will give an 'at risk' score should be administered. This would provide some evidence to help the student and tutor decide whether or not to opt for a full assessment.

Dr Michael Vinegrad's *Adult Dyslexia Checklist* (Adult Dyslexia Organisation) is a user friendly questionnaire and gives a rough and ready guide. It is a quick, non-threatening and easy to use method of self assessment.

The *Dyslexia Adult Screening Test* (Fawcett & Nicolson, 1998) is a much more substantial and reliable screening test. It takes about 35 minutes to administer and gives both a numerical 'at risk quotient' and useful diagnostic information. As well as testing for deficits in the dyslexia sensitive skills of working memory, speed of information processing and phonological awareness, it also gives an indication of a person's non verbal or fluid intelligence, reading and spelling attainment and speed.

Figure 4   **What to look for in dyslexic adults**

a) General Indications

	Yes	No	Sometimes
There will be a gap between general intellectual abilities and basic skills.			
There will be an erratic acquisition of basic skills – they may pick up some ideas extremely quickly, but have great difficulty with others.			
They have good days and bad days – variable performance.			
They learn quickly and they forget quickly.			
They have difficulty with tasks involving short term or working memory and sequencing, e.g. remembering telephone numbers, calculating mental maths, knowing alphabetical order, the order of letters in a word or reading from a calculator.			
Around 80% of dyslexia is genetic, so there are likely to be other people in the family with similar literacy difficulties. The link from father to son is particularly strong.			
They may have difficulty with time estimation and may be late or early for appointments.			
Their organisational skills may be poor, e.g. organising life, files and thoughts on paper.			
They may have problems with balance and co-ordination.			
When talking, they may have word finding difficulties; they know what they want to say, but 'the word won't come' or they'll say the wrong but related word.			
They may have trouble keeping up with the conversation between 4 or 5 friends because of slow language processing speed.			
They might find it difficult to appreciate jokes, a play on words or nuances in language as they tend to take words literally.			
People with dyslexia have many strengths. They may be intuitive and holistic thinkers.			

	Yes	No	Sometimes
• They may have excellent problem solving skills.			
• Their spatial awareness is often good and they are empathetic and creative thinkers.			

b) Literacy Related Difficulties

	Yes	No	Sometimes
• They find it hard to identify and manipulate sounds in words, e.g. being able to generate spoonerisms (fish & chips/chish & fips).			
• If they attempt too many examples of an exercise at one time they will probably get worse. They are not yet automatic, so as soon as they stop thinking about the task, they start to make mistakes.			
• They do not learn efficiently if normal teaching methods are used.			
• They may report that letters or words move or blur when they are reading prose. They may lose their place or miss out words or whole lines.			
• They can unintentionally 'switch off' so that what they are being taught suddenly makes no sense.			
• They may confuse letters similar in shape, e.g. d/p/b/g or m/w and have unreliable letter/sound correspondence.			
• They may mishear, mis-sequence or miss out sounds in words when spelling. Syllables or word endings may be omitted.			
• They may spell the same word differently on the same page without realising and may have difficulty with proofreading if their visual memory for words is weak.			
• When reading, comprehension may be compromised if they are over reliant on decoding.			
• If a motor problem exists, handwriting will be affected. They will have difficulty keeping to the margin and on the line. Letters will be poorly and irregularly constructed and they may report that their hand aches when writing. Articulation might be poor.			
• Copying from the board will be laborious and may be inaccurate.			

Lee, BSA

As learners with dyslexia will need support in accessing some aspects of the Core Curricula, it is extremely important that they are accurately identified and assessed. See *Access for All* (DfES) for guidance.

It is worth remembering also that severe dyslexia is a recognised disability (under the Disability Discrimination Act 1995). Learners may need advice about the help they can get through their Disablement Employment Advisor (DEA) for job finding and the support they can receive through Disabled Students Allowance for higher education courses.

4 How people with dyslexia learn and some of the barriers

'I had it hammered into me at secondary school that I was just factory fodder.'

'This thing (dyslexia) has haunted me all my life.'

ONE of the major barriers to learning that dyslexic adults experience in common with many other adults with basic skills problems, is the horror of placing themselves in a situation where they think they may have these worst fears confirmed.

'It took me ages to pluck up courage to come. There is a big fear of disappointing other people if I can't learn.'

It can take months, and in some cases, years for the individual to take that first step and lay bare to a stranger the secret they have made such strenuous efforts over the years to hide. The relief of finally knowing what the problem is can be overpowering, but can be mixed with feelings of grief, anger, guilt and regret. Many of these conflicting emotions will need to be worked through if the learner is to understand the condition and come to terms with it. It may even be that professional counselling is required. For more information on counselling and dyslexia, see McLoughlin (1994).

Our task as teachers is to demonstrate to dyslexic learners that we understand how dyslexia works and to give them the confidence that, like a certain beer, we will reach the parts that other teachers could not reach . . . and then, of course, we have to make sure that we can!

An appreciation of the particular learning styles common to most dyslexic learners will help us adapt our teaching style (see Figure 5). Figure 6 outlines good practice for dyslexia teachers.

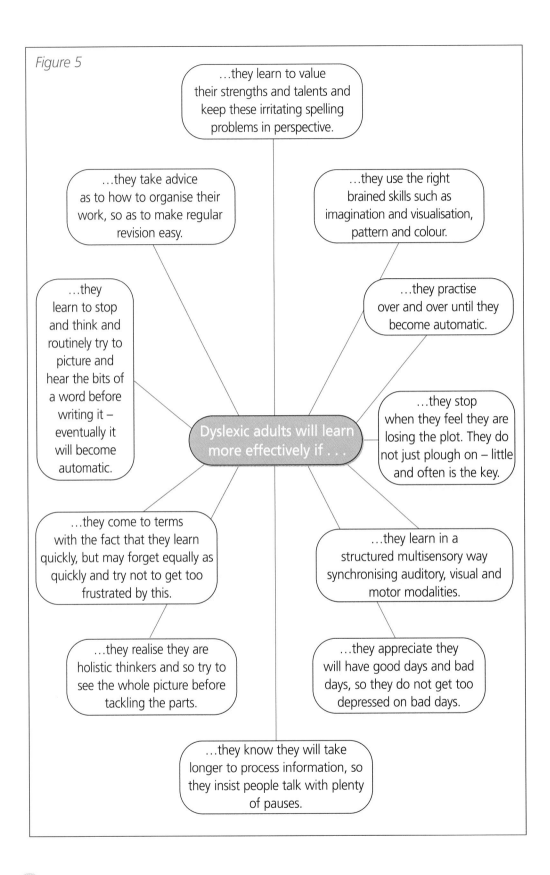

Figure 5

...they learn to value their strengths and talents and keep these irritating spelling problems in perspective.

...they take advice as to how to organise their work, so as to make regular revision easy.

...they use the right brained skills such as imagination and visualisation, pattern and colour.

...they learn to stop and think and routinely try to picture and hear the bits of a word before writing it – eventually it will become automatic.

...they practise over and over until they become automatic.

Dyslexic adults will learn more effectively if . . .

...they stop when they feel they are losing the plot. They do not just plough on – little and often is the key.

...they come to terms with the fact that they learn quickly, but may forget equally as quickly and try not to get too frustrated by this.

...they learn in a structured multisensory way synchronising auditory, visual and motor modalities.

...they realise they are holistic thinkers and so try to see the whole picture before tackling the parts.

...they appreciate they will have good days and bad days, so they do not get too depressed on bad days.

...they know they will take longer to process information, so they insist people talk with plenty of pauses.

Figure 6

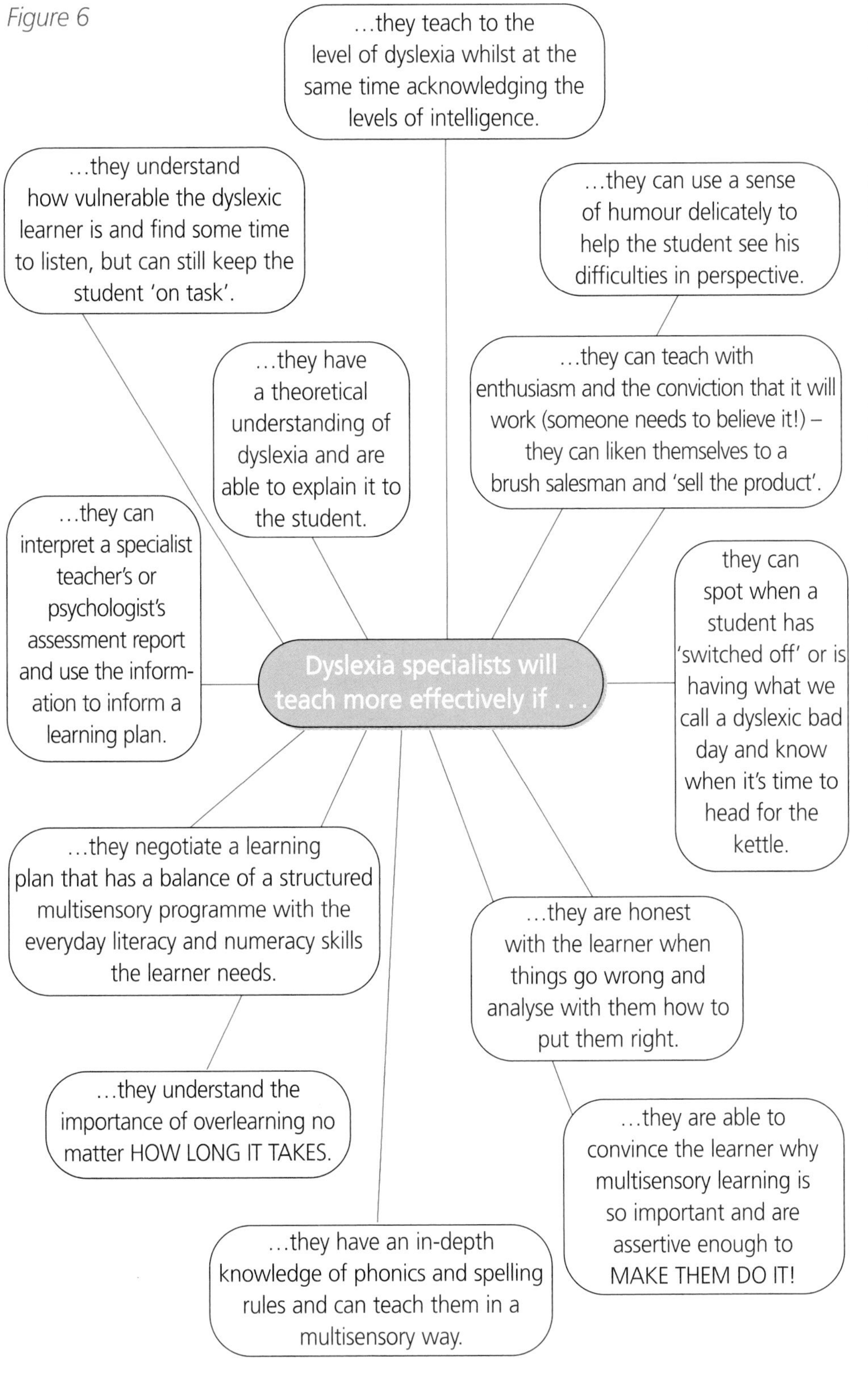

...they teach to the level of dyslexia whilst at the same time acknowledging the levels of intelligence.

...they understand how vulnerable the dyslexic learner is and find some time to listen, but can still keep the student 'on task'.

...they can use a sense of humour delicately to help the student see his difficulties in perspective.

...they have a theoretical understanding of dyslexia and are able to explain it to the student.

...they can teach with enthusiasm and the conviction that it will work (someone needs to believe it!) – they can liken themselves to a brush salesman and 'sell the product'.

...they can interpret a specialist teacher's or psychologist's assessment report and use the information to inform a learning plan.

Dyslexia specialists will teach more effectively if . . .

they can spot when a student has 'switched off' or is having what we call a dyslexic bad day and know when it's time to head for the kettle.

...they negotiate a learning plan that has a balance of a structured multisensory programme with the everyday literacy and numeracy skills the learner needs.

...they are honest with the learner when things go wrong and analyse with them how to put them right.

...they understand the importance of overlearning no matter HOW LONG IT TAKES.

...they are able to convince the learner why multisensory learning is so important and are assertive enough to MAKE THEM DO IT!

...they have an in-depth knowledge of phonics and spelling rules and can teach them in a multisensory way.

Once the dyslexic learner is in a teaching situation that is appropriate for his needs, many of the barriers to learning will begin to fall away. However dyslexia bites deep and sometimes a small failure or an unguarded comment will bring all the old feelings back.

As Clive says, in another extract from his poem *Dyslexia*:

'Only myself to blame
A life sentence,
My heart sobs at the news
I am a prisoner for a crime I have not committed
Will I ever be a free man?'

And one of our talented teachers who has dyslexia herself, says:

'You don't expect to be valued.'

These barriers to learning; the lack of self esteem, shame, embarrassment, feelings of failure, anger, frustration, guilt, fear and lack of confidence are common, we know, to many basic skills students, but can be heightened with dyslexic students. Carefully planned and sensitively delivered specialist teaching which takes into account the general dyslexic learning styles and his own individual learning styles, will eventually prove to the student that he can succeed.

As one learner wrote when asked to evaluate his first course of specialist teaching:

'when I started here, Jenny said you will by writing
sentences soon. I thought yes and pigs might fly.
Thank you very mush for proving me wrog.'

(sic)

How the Curriculum does and does not work for dyslexic learners

THE *Adult Literacy Core Curriculum* has been designed to enable the learner to develop a range of strategies or searchlights, each of which, when working properly, will shed some light on the text.

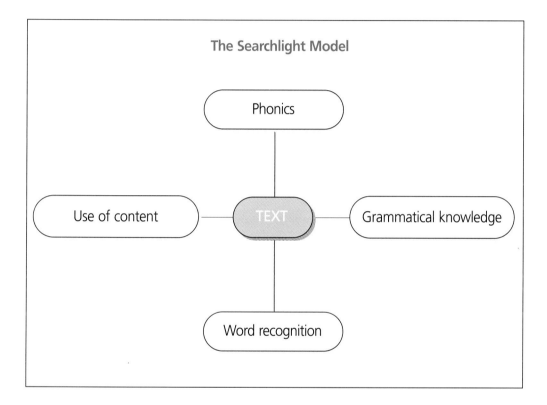

The Searchlight Model

Phonics

Use of content — TEXT — Grammatical knowledge

Word recognition

To continue the analogy, if one or more of these searchlights is switched off or is dim, then there will be less illumination upon the text. In other words, fluent reading with understanding or fluent writing will be less likely to occur. The fewer searchlights that are shining brightly, the more dependent a learner will be on the remaining one/s. For instance, a learner with poor phonic skills will over-rely on the context, whole word recognition and syntax. Conversely, a learner with poor visual memory for whole words might rely too much on phonics and lose the meaning.

Our aim, as teachers, is to ensure all these searchlights are switched on and polished.

In order to be able to analyse the efficiency of these searchlights and teach learners to use them systematically, the *National Standards for Adult Literacy* are divided into:

- text focus skills
    - deriving meaning when reading
    - using different styles when writing

- sentence focus skills
    - grammar
    - sentence structure
    - punctuation

- word focus skills
    - phonics and phonological awareness
    - structure and pattern
    - whole word recognition.

Any teaching of reading and spelling should, whenever possible, draw on all three focuses simultaneously. (See the *Adult Literacy Core Curriculum*, introduction p. 7-8.)

The Curriculum gives an extremely valuable insight into teaching and learning which enhances the work of the dyslexia specialist. By seeing the whole picture, we can begin to make judgements as to which of the searchlights and focuses need the most input when helping dyslexic learners. When we use this model, we will be less likely to teach at one focus and neglect the others.

For the first time in adult literacy teaching, we have a national structure which we can use as a framework for planning our teaching. This, in itself, is a great step forward for dyslexic learners who need structure and order in their learning.

The DfES has now published *Access for All* (2002) which provides further support and advice on using the Core Curricula with learners with dyslexia.

The Problem of Word Level Skills

With most adult dyslexic learners, it is the word level skills that cause the greatest problem and these, if not addressed properly, will have an impact on text level skills. Inefficient decoding and poor sight reading of words compromises the higher level comprehension skills; similarly laboured encoding when spelling reduces the ability to release the higher level thought processes needed for creating fluent writing.

There will, therefore, need to be a much greater emphasis than is necessary for other basic skills learners on developing these vital word level skills. Difficulties in this area can act like a cork in a wine bottle, blocking the facility for the dyslexic person to use his innate intelligence and skills for reading and writing. You cannot delight in the wine until the cork has been removed. Word level deficits block the facility to enjoy the higher order reading and writing skills.

'I have a great understanding of words and language and yet I can find it impossible sometimes to spell a word that has only three letters in it. With all the effort I can muster, I dredge the very deepest parts of my mind; sometimes it seems as if my head will explode with the effort, yet I cannot find or hear or see the sound of the word that has three letters. No one who has not got dyslexia will ever know how it makes me feel. It's sometimes unbearable, it rocks the very foundations of my life.'

Sometimes word level skills will have to be taught in isolation, so that there are enough opportunities for systematic overlearning (remember it may be up to 100 times more than for non dyslexic learners). However, the words to be learnt should always arise out of the learner's needs as identified from the text and should, once learned, be transferred back into text through reading and writing.

There may also be a problem in the Curriculum when similar phonic patterns are grouped too closely together for spelling. This, strangely does not seem to cause so much of a problem when reading. For instance, a dyslexic student can learn that when reading, 'ir', 'ur', 'er' and 'ear' they may all sound (er), but they would experience enormous confusion if these graphemes were taught close to each other as spelling choices. Different spelling choices for a single phoneme should preferably be taught weeks apart, so that each one is well established before a new one is introduced. If the pace is too brisk, the result will be partly learnt and partly forgotten spellings. With severely dyslexic adults, no matter how intelligent they are, each phonic pattern will need to be taught explicitly as a unit, thoroughly practised at word and sentence levels, then reinforced at text level.

Sentence and Text Levels

On the whole, the sentence and text level skills present less of a problem for the dyslexia specialist and can be taught much as suggested in the Curriculum. However, as mentioned earlier, at text level, comprehension skills may be weak because of poorly established word level skills and memory problems. When this is the case extra multisensory strategies will be needed to address this problem. Similarly, when writing, the dyslexic learner may need additional strategies to help with organisational skills.

The *Adult Literacy Core Curriculum* stresses the importance of metacognition (learning about learning and being aware of the purpose of learning).

> *'It is important that the learner is clear about what they are learning and what the activities they are undertaking are designed to teach.'*
>
> (*Adult Literacy Core Curriculum* p.9)

6 Different approaches within the dyslexic continuum

IT will be evident to any tutor who has worked with dyslexic learners that, unfortunately, no two students show the same type or degree of dyslexia; nor do they have the same learning styles or the same needs and priorities. This, of course, holds true for all basic skills learners, but with dyslexic learners we need to be very careful to identify how severely dyslexic they are and which particular modality has been most affected. For instance, is it mainly a phonological problem, or are there visual perceptual problems and motor control difficulties as well? Sometimes it can be a combination of two or all three. Almost always there will be problems with memory and developing automaticity. Sometimes speed of processing information will be slow.

Our next task will be to assess exactly which word level skills the student possesses. A reliable reading and spelling test such as the *Wide Range Achievement Test* (1998), which is standardised for adults, will give a percentile and standard score. This can sometimes help the tutor to decide with the learner how structured the reading and spelling programme will need to be. Diagnostic information can be gathered from this and a piece of free writing using Cynthia Klein's diagnostic spelling analysis (*Diagnosing Dyslexia*, 1993).

Further spelling analysis can be done by giving a structured spelling test based on the order in which phonics and spelling rules are introduced in the Curriculum. Word attack and sight reading skills for reading can be estimated using tests of irregular and non words (Klein, 1993).

As with all basic skills learners, it is important to find out at which level of the National Standards they are functioning at text, sentence and word level. Some tests for word level skills have been described above. Sentence and text level skills can be determined by using some of the exercises described in the Curriculum or by carrying out a free writing analysis or a miscue analysis of reading (Klein, 1993).

For more information about assessing dyslexic students in higher education, see Singleton (1999) and in a basic skills setting, see Lee's chapter on Adult Dyslexia in Townend & Turner (2000).

Many students, but particularly dyslexic learners will show a 'spiky' profile of skills. The chart overleaf will help both learner and tutor to see the pattern of strengths and weaknesses. The Curriculum levels are broad and it should not be assumed that a learner will necessarily move from level to level in a year, so movement within a level can also be plotted.

Figure 7   **Mapping against the Standards**

Learner's Name: ....

	Reading			Writing		
	Text level	Sentence level	Word level	Text level	Sentence level	Word level
Entry 1						
Entry 2						
Entry 3						
Level 1						
Level 2						

Start of course	S	Date: ....
End of course	E	Date: ....

Figure 7 can be photocopied without prior permission of the Basic Skills Agency, for educational purposes only.

Figure 8 shows a typical spiky profile that might be seen with a dyslexic learner. Note the relatively weak word level skills compared to the stronger text level skills.

Figure 8   **Learner Profile**

Learner's Name: ....

	Reading			Writing		
	Text level	Sentence level	Word level	Text level	Sentence level	Word level
Entry 1						
Entry 2						S / E
Entry 3		S	S / E			
Level 1	S	E		S	S	
Level 2	E			E	E	

Start of course	S	Date: ....
End of course	E	Date: ....

(Data from these charts may also be useful when compiling statistics for a local and national picture of adults' basic skills.)

Once an analysis of the learner's difficulties has been carried out and Curriculum levels established, his preferred learning styles may be determined through questioning, information from the assessment, trial and error, observation and perhaps the use of a questionnaire.

All this data, together with information on the learner's own personal goals, the time he has at his disposal, his priorities and the materials available, can now be used to develop a learning plan.

As can be seen from the chart of a dyslexic learner on page 29, the teacher will be working at different Curriculum levels for word, sentence and text focus.

At this stage, decisions will have to be made as to whether the learner needs greater emphasis on what I call the *'sticking plaster approach'*, in other words how to use technology to override his urgent literacy problems, or the *'antibiotic approach'*, where a more leisurely and measured programme of work can be designed to begin to 'cure' the spelling or reading difficulties. Usually a combination of both is required.

Be aware that the dyslexic learner may additionally need help to develop phonological awareness, memory and organisational skills, although phonological awareness activities will probably only be necessary for people who have a phonological dyslexia and have very low literacy skills.

Choosing a Programme of Work

1. *Severely Dyslexic Learners*

Assuming then that the antibiotic approach will be used to a greater or lesser extent, a severely dyslexic learner who will almost certainly have phonological dyslexia will need to develop his word and sentence level skills through a highly structured multisensory phonic programme.

When working on this programme, he will be taught to look at letters or words, at the same time saying them out loud. He must then repeat them, picturing them in his mind's eye, then finally he must write them, saying the letter names as he writes. This multisensory approach which engages the Broca's and Wernicke's areas of the brain simultaneously (see Chapter 2) may sound enormously tedious, but it soon becomes second nature to both student and tutor and most importantly, it works! Examples of these programmes include Cathy Diggle's *Write/Right to Read*, the Dyslexia Institute's *Dyslexia Institute Literacy Programme* (restricted use) and Walter Bramley's *Units of Sound*. It is advisable to organise training for the teachers who are going to deliver these specialist programmes, as they are only effective if used in a full multisensory way.

Programmes such as these will not of course address all of the severely dyslexic learner's needs. He will also need a way of spelling the words he needs most urgently. One tried and tested method of doing this is MUSP (*The Multisensory Spelling Programme for Priority Words*, Lee, 2000 in Townend & Turner) which will be described later in this book (see Chapter 8 and Appendix 3). Work on priority words is shown in the *Adult Literacy Core Curriculum* at word level from Entry 1 to Level 1 (Ww/E1.1&3, Ww/E2.1&2, Ww/E3.1&2 and Ww/L1.1). Dyslexic learners will also need multisensory help with general functional literacy tasks such as letter writing and form filling as well as advice on developing reading comprehension skills. (See Chapter 10.) For further advice and guidance see information box 'Multisensory Approaches to Teaching' in *Access for All* (DfES, 2002).

2. Moderately Dyslexic Learners

Moderately dyslexic learners will not need such a structured programme and their word level needs may be addressed by linking spelling activities and exercises to the Curriculum phonics guide or perhaps the *LEAP Fast Track Spelling Programme* spelling order (see Lee, 2000 and Turner, 2000 – Appendix 1).

Walter Bramley's *Literacy for Study and Work, Alpha to Omega* (Hornsby) and Elizabeth Wood's *Exercise Your Spelling* are examples of the many spelling books that can be used to practise spellings once a structure has been agreed. MUSP can be used as a way of attacking important personal words. Also see information box 'Using an individualised spelling programme' in *Access for All*.

More advanced sentence and text level skills will need to be taught together with memory strategies and organisational skills. Again, personal literacy problems such as reading instructions at work or helping with the children's homework will also need to be addressed in a multisensory way.

3. Mildly Dyslexic Learners

Mildly dyslexic learners may still need a way of learning how to spell special interest words. Again, MUSP *(The Multisensory Spelling Programme for Priority Words)* can be used together with some tuition on selected spelling rules and patterns, but they may also need to concentrate more on multisensory study skills, higher level reading and writing skills or report writing for work. They will be able to access the Curriculum more readily, but care should be taken even at this level to include plenty of overlearning.

All dyslexic learners should be encouraged to develop word processing skills. In our experience, this is one of the main keys to success, particularly in higher education, where even severely dyslexic students can gain good degrees if they are computer literate. For more information see information box 'Using a word processor' in *Access for All*.

ALL good learning plans grow out of assessment, the identification of needs, the student's goals, learning styles and priorities and the time he has available. They should now take into account the new Curriculum and Standards.

This assessment and planning stage takes time and should not be rushed. Time spent at this stage enhances the quality of teaching later.

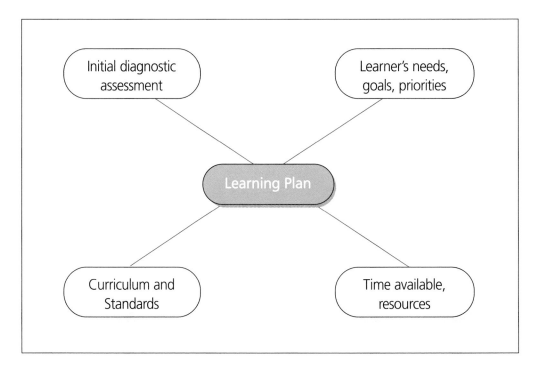

The Core Curriculum is clear about the importance of planning relevant learning activities.

> *'This Adult Literacy Core Curriculum provides the skills framework, the learner provides the context and the tutor needs to bring them together in a learning programme.'*
>
> (Curriculum introduction p.9)

There are many different ways of drawing up a learning plan and life would be very boring (though possibly less stressful during inspection) if they were all the same. Providing the learning plan includes the following components in whatever form of words seems appropriate, it will meet the needs of the student.

Figure 9　　　　　　　**COMPONENTS OF A LEARNING PLAN**

Learner's Name: ....　　Date: ....

Timescale: ....

Aims　　　　　– What do I want to achieve?

　　　　　　　　– Long and shorter term

Objectives　　– How am I going to achieve it?

　　　　　　　　(Here, we are unpacking the skills required and the steps needed to achieve these goals – these need to be specific, measurable, achievable, realistic and time bound – SMART.)

Existing Skills – What I can do already in these areas/what Curriculum levels am I working at? (if not stated elsewhere)

Materials　　　– What I will need to facilitate learning?

Priorities　　　– What needs tackling most urgently?

Signatures　　– of both student and tutor

This obviously applies to all basic skills learners, but overleaf (Figure 10) is an example of how we would plan with a dyslexic learner so that his achievements could be measured at review.

Figure 10   **SAMPLE LEARNING PLAN FOR A DYSLEXIC LEARNER**

Name: Barry   **Timescale:** From September 19 to July 17

a) Long term aims: To be able to write without feeling embarrassed. To cope better with my job.

b) Short term aims: What I need/want to learn.

1. Improve reading and spelling using a structured language programme (Write/Right to Read)

2. Develop multisensory strategies for learning priority words for report forms

3. Be able to read and understand instructions for machinery at work

4. Be able to record phone numbers accurately

5. Be able to act upon verbal instructions given by the doctor

c) Existing Skills: Confident in writing cvc words but unsure of some blends & vowel sounds. Good at visualising things. Can read machinery instructions slowly but forgets what has read.

Word level skills: Spelling – Entry 1, Reading – Entry 2

Text level skills: Writing – Entry 2, Reading – Entry 3

Sentence level skills: Writing – Entry 2, Reading – Entry 3

d) What I will do to achieve these aims:

1.1   Feel confident in spelling and reading all words up to Module 5 in Write/Right to Read

1.2   Have a good grasp of basic language terminology e.g. definition of vowels, consonant, open and closed syllables, suffixes, phonemes. Be able to read and spell words using the 'vccv' pattern

2.   Be able to spell confidently and in context 25 priority words using the MUSP system

3.1   Be able to skim to gain an overview of the machine instructions

3.2   Sight read all difficult words in the instruction manual by using flashcards

3.3   Learn how to split up the long words in the instruction manual into base word, suffix and syllables to help decoding

3.4 Create mental pictures of how to carry out the instructions

4   Improve accuracy by chunking, picturing, sub vocalising and proofreading phone numbers

5.1 Feel confident enough to ask the doctor to repeat instructions or write them down

5.2 Use 'rehearsal' skills to remember them by repeating them in my head

5.3 Find ways of writing in note form to aid memory

e) What are the priorities?   Reading and understanding machine instructions

f) What about materials and methods?   Write/Right to Read Modules 1-5, MUSP (Multisensory Spelling Programme for Priority Words), blank report sheets from work, copy of machine operating instructions, word processor. Use role play for phone calls and listening to instructions.

g) We will review your progress together after about 6 hours then 36 hours.

Would you prefer to review more often? No

You are entitled to at least 4 hours tuition per week.

Everyone involved in this centre will be respected and appreciated, irrespective of gender, race, culture, age and ability.

Signed .... (student)

Signed .... (tutor)

Notice on the learning plan how the numbering system in section b) relates to the numbering in section d). If the same numbering system is used when reviewing learning, then it is easy to measure progress against the precise objectives in section d).

By using multisensory learning techniques, we are optimising our chances of using the learner's strengths whilst at the same time working on his weaker modality.

Our aim when planning learning is to have high expectations of our learners and to be aware of their potential, whilst at the same time being realistic as to the amount of overlearning that is required for mastery.

8 Word level skills

*'I have had about 20 jobs, saiting around the wold
driving arown Europ…but if only I could spel? . . .'*

(sic)

*'The worst thing is the feeling of not being in control,
having to get help from other pepel.'*

(sic)

WORD level skills underpin all literacy teaching and they comprise two of our four searchlights. Good readers and writers ensure phonic and sight reading skills interact with semantic and syntactic skills to result in the continuous monitoring of the text.

As we know, most dyslexic learners find word level skills to be their greatest problem and often tutors find them the most difficult to teach.

When we are deciding on which words to learn, we will take examples from the text and once learnt, apply them to the text.

There are 4 main strands to teaching word level skills.

1. The teaching of phonology and phonological awareness leading to the development of the phonic skills of blending (spelling) and/or decoding (reading).

2. Working on spelling rules and logic, e.g. understanding the principles of syllable division, how to add suffixes and understanding spelling patterns.

3. The development of a visual memory for shapes of letters and whole words.

4. Learning how to choose effective spelling strategies and systems for learning priority words.

It is important that we do not concentrate on just one of these areas, but teach all. We should show the learners how to integrate them and how to choose the best approach for the word to be learnt.

We should always integrate the teaching of spelling with reading where appropriate (see p.8 of the *Adult Literacy Core Curriculum*).

1. Using a Phonic Approach

This is often the dyslexic learner's weakest modality, but it would be an unwise teacher who ignored it and worked only to the student's strengths. The whole purpose of multisensory teaching is that by using the learner's strengths, we strengthen the weaknesses.

Visual strategies alone have only limited value. It is very difficult to generate an unknown spelling or read new words from first principles, if there is not a sound phonic foundation.

Students who do not have phonic skills find it difficult to move completely out of Frith's logographic stage into the alphabetic stage (see Figure 11).

Figure 11   **Summary of Frith's model for the normal development of reading and writing skills**

Logographic Phase

* Whole words recognised for reading, but cannot decode, e.g. can read 'McDonalds' but not 'trend'

* Very little, if any, letter/sound correspondence so spelling can be 'bizarre'

Alphabetic Phase

* Can now decode regular words when reading where there is direct letter/sound correspondence, e.g. can read 'splint' but not 'yacht'

* Can spell by mapping sounds directly onto letters, e.g. 'yoos' for 'for use' and 'apsoloot' for 'absolute'

Orthographic Phase

* Can recognise letter strings, e.g. 'tion' saying (sh'n) or 'ove' saying (uv)

* Combines logographic and alphabetic skills to tackle irregular or long words

* Can spell by analogy e.g. if 'picture' then 'lecture'. Can use spelling rules, e.g. hit + ing = hitting

---

In the very first stages of teaching phonics (see *Adult Literacy Core Curriculum* Ww/E1.2&3), it is important to establish some basic terminology.

- Teach the difference between letter names and letter sounds.

- When dealing with consonant sounds, make it clear which are the voiced and which the unvoiced consonant sounds, for instance, 'm', 'l' and 'n' (mm, ll & nn, not muh, luh and nuh) are voiced whereas 's', 't' and 'p' are unvoiced (you cannot hear your voice at all when you say these sounds).

- Help learners to discriminate between long and short vowel sounds.

- Enable learners to say letter sounds accurately by feeling them in their mouths (use a mirror if necessary) and analysing what their mouths are doing (tongue, lips, teeth) as they are saying the sounds.

- Give definitions of vowels, consonants, syllables, suffixes and phonemes. Definitions can be given on small cards so that the student is able to practise them until he knows them.

These are the bricks and mortar of language teaching.

With dyslexic learners at a basic level of literacy, it will often be necessary to integrate phonological awareness exercises such as the ones described in Appendix 2 into a structured multisensory phonic teaching programme such as Write/Right to Read. If the tutor has no access to such a programme, it is possible to use the order for introducing phonics in the *Adult Literacy Core Curriculum* as a basis for the phonic programme. They are found in the Curriculum at word level at Entry 1 (Ww/E1.3) and are built up incrementally throughout the levels at Entry 2 and 3 (Ww/E2.2 and Ww/E3.2). It is using the knowledge from the development of these skills which helps learners to spell a more complex and greater range of words. For further information see the information box 'Role of phonics' in *Access for All*.

Each phoneme, with its corresponding letter or letters (grapheme) and each blend will need to be introduced separately then read and written in words and sentences. Care will need to be taken during this part of the lesson, never to give a learner any words, sentences or texts to work on which contain sounds that have not been explicitly taught. Cards containing the phonemes, blends and word chunks can be given to the learner to practise, so that he is able to give an automatic response to these given letters or sounds. For instance, at a later stage in the programme, when seeing the letters 'tion' on a card, he should be able to respond automatically 'sh'n' and when hearing the sound 'sh'n' at the end of a word he should know instantly that the first spelling choice would be 'tion'. Eventually he will be given 'sion' and 'cian'. These card packs will grow as the student progresses through the phonic programme of the Curriculum. All the phonic patterns described in the four boxes on pages 107, 113, 119 and 125 of the *Adult Literacy Core Curriculum* can be put onto reading and spelling cards to develop automaticity.

All teaching on this phonic programme should be multisensory. This involves learners having to say words and then letter names out loud as they see them and as they write them. This could well lead to initial resistance from the learner! This is the time when the explanations about brain activity prove useful. If dyslexic students understand why you are asking them to learn in this strange way, you have a marginally better chance of their doing so. Occasionally it may be worth letting them find out how much less effective learning is if they do not use multisensory methods. Even with the explanations, regular good humoured reminders will be needed because of memory problems.

Figure 12 **Multisensory Spelling – a student's guide**

1. You *see* the word on the page.
   You *say* it – *feeling* it in your mouth
   and at the same time *hearing* it.

2. You cover the word, *say* it and *hear* it whilst *picturing* it, bit by bit in your mind's eye.

3. Now you *write* it as you *say* it – you *see* it, *say* it, *hear* it and *feel* it.

4. You *check* it letter by letter with the original to see if it is correct.

You will find that if you integrate all these modalities each time you learn the word, when you come to write it in a report or essay, if one modality fails then one of the others takes over.

For instance, if you can not remember what the word looks like, you will remember hearing yourself saying it. If both those strategies fail, the word will probably be 'in your hand' and you will just be able to write it.

---

1. Working on Spelling Rules and Logic

For a dyslexic learner who does not automatically spell many words, access to rules and logic which will help him work them out from first principles can be his salvation. CVC words are introduced in the Curriculum at Entry 1 (Rw/E1.2 and Ww/E1.3). Incremental work on adding suffixes is developed at Entry 2 and 3 (Ww/E2.2 and Ww/E3.3).

Because dyslexic adults are often holistic thinkers, it is usually a good idea to take them quickly through a piece of spelling logic so that they can see where it is heading before starting to work on each stage.

There are many fascinating spelling rules and logical methods for spelling which good spellers have either never needed to learn or have long since forgotten. Dyslexic students might need them for a long time and they will be understood very quickly by a bright dyslexic adult. However, if not practised over and over again, they will be forgotten equally as quickly.

It has often been said that dyslexic people are *not* 'slow learners', but *are* 'quick forgetters'. This is because they need much more practice than non-dyslexic learners to achieve automaticity.

Spelling Safely With Syllables in Appendix 4 shows how you can take some simple ideas and develop them to be able to work out the spellings of a wide range of words. Much practice will be needed at each stage.

This spelling logic uses the dyslexic adult's intellectual strengths and addresses some of the spelling rules from Entry to Level 2. It is written for dyslexic learners rather than tutors and can be photocopied.

2. Developing a Visual Memory for Words

Most dyslexic students can be taught to remember words visually for reading, if words are written clearly on small flash cards and are actively practised using simple games such as pairs or pelmanism.

Rapid Read is a useful game for reinforcing visual memory, but only use games if all the learners feel comfortable with them and they meet the teaching objectives.

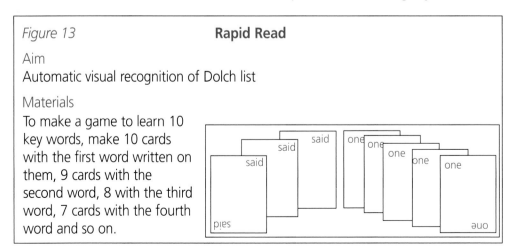

Figure 13　　　　　　　　　　**Rapid Read**

Aim
Automatic visual recognition of Dolch list

Materials
To make a game to learn 10 key words, make 10 cards with the first word written on them, 9 cards with the second word, 8 with the third word, 7 cards with the fourth word and so on.

Method

Shuffle the cards and deal each player two cards which he places face up on the table. Place the pack face down.

The first player picks up a card from the pack and says the word. He can take a matching card from any other player. The play continues until all the pack is used up. The person with the most cards is the winner. It is a fast moving game with rapid changes of fortune and dozens of opportunities to LOOK AND SAY.

Developing a visual memory for spelling is sometimes not so easy because every letter must be accurately mapped. To do this with the dyslexic learner, the full multisensory approach should be employed to create what we call the Mind's Eye Spelling technique.

Figure 14   **Minds's Eye Spelling**

Write the word you want to spell both as a whole word in joined up writing and also split into chunks.

        cirrhosis   *ci rr hosis*

Say the whole word, then say the chunks.

        'cirrhosis'   *'c i double r hosis'*

Now cover them, say the word and the strategy (the chunks). As you say the strategy, picture each little bit in your mind's eye.

        'cirrhosis'   *'c i double r hosis'*

Next, look at that word in your mind's eye and answer some questions about it.

      What's the middle chunk?   *(double r)*
      What letter comes after the 'h'?   *(o)*
      What letter comes before the 'h'?   *(r)* etc.

Spell it, saying the letter names, by reading it off from your mind's eye.

          c – i – r – r – h – o – s – i – s

Spell it backwards by reading it off. (This is often surprisingly easy to do even for dyslexic learners!)

          s – i – s – o – h – r – r – i – c

Write it as a whole word in joined up writing by saying each chunk as you write it.

      'c - i double r hosis'   *cirrhosis*

Check, letter by letter with the original and amaze your friends at dinner parties!

Students can rarely picture a whole word straight away, but they can usually be trained to build it up in their mind's eye by simultaneously activating the auditory and visual centres in the language area of the brain.

The need to use visual strategies is introduced in the Curriculum at Entry 2 (Ww/E2.1 p.110). This is how to make it work with dyslexic learners.

4. Spelling Priority Words Using MUSP (Multisensory Spelling Programme for Priority Words)

Even when teaching a highly structured specialist programme, there is always a need for a learner to be able to spell urgently the words he needs for work, study or home. It is no good saying 'we will teach you these when we reach Module 15 in eighteen months time', or trying to dot about the programme to find the appropriate rule. The first option will result in exasperation and the second in confusion.

We need a method for teaching these groups of words systematically and separately from the structured programme.

The author devised MUSP (Multisensory Spelling Programme for Priority Words, see Appendix 3) to address these problems systematically so that automaticity is obtained. In informal surveys of this programme, we have shown-long term benefits with success rates of between 80 – 97%. It has proved to be one of the most useful methods we have found for a dyslexic learner to address some of the word level skills at Entry 1 ('important personal words', Curriculum p.106) and Entry 3 ('know and understand their own preferred strategies to expanding spelling confidence', Curriculum p.118), but it can be used at all levels of the Curriculum.

Because it is wholly multisensory, it acts as a catch-all for both visual and auditory learners and, because it builds in a great deal of overlearning, it ensures automaticity. It also encourages the learner to integrate reading and spelling skills, develop his own best learning strategies and become more independent.

Some important points to remember when using MUSP

MUSP (see Appendix 3), is written for students and can be photocopied.

1. It is extremely important to follow MUSP exactly as suggested. Short cuts with the multisensory routine or spending less than the minimum 4 weeks (you can spend longer) on each list will result in disappointment. It may be tempting to move on to a new list before the end of the allotted 4 weeks when a learner insists he knows the words, but, if he is dyslexic, he will not yet be automatic, even if he thinks he is, and moving on too early will result in words half learnt and half forgotten.

2. Note also how important it is to carry out every step in the *'look, say – cover, picture and say – write, say – check'* routine. The step that tends to be left out is step 2 *'cover, picture and say'* (the mind's eye bit), because once the word is covered, the learner is anxious to write it down 'before I forget'. This stage is *the* most important one because during this process the learner is committing the word into both auditory and visual memory.

3. The learner should always say the whole word and immediately after say the strategy. This is because when he is writing an essay or report that contains that word, the whole word will come into his head and, if this process is used, the strategy will automatically 'click in'.

4. The MUSP programme is designed so that systematic overlearning is built in (with dyslexia you can afford to leave nothing to chance!) Make sure the student proofreads his spellings after he has been tested, but before checking with the original by saying the strategy and seeing if what he has written fits the strategy. He will not have the original at work, so he needs an independent way of checking.

Once both teacher and learner are confident that the correct processes are being used, MUSP can be carried out by the student independently. Almost all learners who have used MUSP have found it to be the most effective way they have encountered to learn these special interest words.

A word about handwriting

Most dyslexia specialists agree that the motor or muscle memory for words is easier to develop if a learner writes using joined up writing. (Try closing your eyes and writing your name and address in print and then in joined up writing.) It is worth encouraging dyslexic students to use joined up writing. Explain to them how motor memory can be the most powerful memory for words because once the word is 'in the hand' it is truly automatic.

Word processing skills are also important and all dyslexic learners should have the opportunity to learn these skills. Some dyslexic students come to rely on word processing for almost all their written language and this is as reasonable as a person with poor eyesight relying on glasses.

Developing a wider vocabulary

Most students at college or university find they will suddenly need to be able to read, spell and understand the meanings of a great number of new words. By using a similar system to MUSP they will find they can do this quite easily (Figure 15).

Make 3 columns on the page and label them as follows.

Whole word	The word in chunks and how it sounds	What it means
1. cirque	cir que (sir k)	a deep bow shaped hollow at the head of a valley
2. etc.		
3.		
4.		

The student should be able to work on about 10 words at a time.

He should read each word out loud, read aloud the strategy for spelling, then read aloud the meaning.

Next, he should cover the line and say all three from memory.

Then he should write the word as a whole word, saying the strategy as he writes it.

During the learning period (again a minimum of 4 weeks) ask the student to make a conscious effort to spot the words he is learning in any texts he is reading and use the words in sentences and, of course, in his writing.

The sticking plaster approach

All the suggestions in this chapter so far have been concerned with our 'antibiotic' approach, but for reasons such as time, or degree of dyslexia, more instant solutions may be needed for these difficulties with word level skills. Its always a good idea to address a problem from as many angles as possible, so introduce students to electronic spellchecks and thesauruses, laptops and PCs at an early stage. Many dyslexic learners find the voice activated software very useful, although it does take time to train the computer to the individual's voice. A useful guide, *IT for Dyslexic Adults* by Carol Kaufman can be obtained from the British Dyslexia Association (see also the section on resources in *Access for All*).

Word level skills are the basic building blocks of language. By experimenting with a range of strategies and approaches, the dyslexic adult will begin to develop independence and confidence in this, his most troublesome area.

A definition of a sentence, such as the one given in the schools' National Curriculum document, can be a starting point for sentence level work.

> *'A sentence starts with a capital letter; ends with a*
> *full stop and makes complete sense.'*

Sentence level skills will start to be addressed at Entry 1 (Rs/E1 p.56, Ws/E1 p.104).

As with other definitions, this particular one for a sentence can go on to a small card for the learner to practise and remember, then he can try identifying and highlighting sentences in a piece of text. Sentence level skills can be far less of a problem than word level skills to many dyslexic learners and many of the sentence level activities described in the Curriculum are perfectly suitable for dyslexic learners. It is not a good idea, however, to give them muddled sentences to sort out.

Some dyslexic learners may need a lot of experience with simple sentences. Definitions of verbs, nouns, adjectives etc. can be given on definition cards for reference.

Showing students how to expand a simple sentence in a structured way will help them to create compound and complex sentences that make grammatical sense.

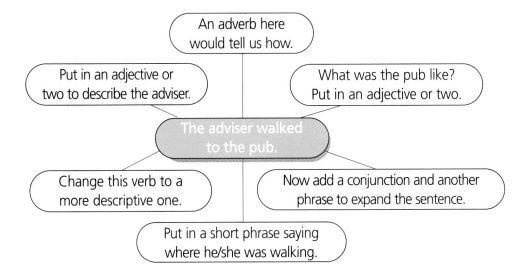

They will learn the power of words if they practise expanding simple sentences to create different effects. For instance, ask learners to expand the same sentence again, this time with words that mean the opposite of the ones they originally chose. Give them practice in joining short sentences using connectives to make long ones, and splitting long sentences into short ones.

This work reflects the Curriculum activities at Entry 3 (Ws/E3.1 p.116).

Much of the punctuation work can be begun orally. It is much easier to tell when a sentence is or is not a question, or exactly which parts of a sentence require commas or speech marks, if the student first says the sentence out loud.

Word classes can be reinforced by highlighting in different colours all the verbs, nouns, adjectives, adverbs etc. in a piece of text. They can then be collected in columns labelled verb, noun etc., then recombined to form different sentences.

'The brilliant adviser trailed wearily along the long dark road
to the dingy pub after he had spent a frustrating day
irritably filling in countless forms.'

Nouns	Verbs	Adjectives	Pronouns	Adverbs
adviser	trailed	brilliant	he	wearily
road	had spent	dark		irritably
pub	filling	dingy		
forms		countless		
day		frustrating		
		long		

Strategies for developing basic sentences into more mature forms can be given by showing learners how to use pronouns and conjunctions and how to change the order of phrases, e.g:

1. 'My name is Janet. I have a husband and three children. I live in Teesdale. I like cooking, watching TV and hang-gliding. My husband's name is Dave. Dave works shifts. Dave can look after the kids at weekends.'

2. 'My name is Janet. My husband, three children and I live in Teesdale. At weekends I go hang-gliding, but I also enjoy cooking and watching TV. My husband Dave works shifts so he can look after the kids at weekends.'

For more ideas, see also the Literacy Curriculum Wt/L1 p.122 & 123. As stated in the Curriculum (p.105), 'Beginning writers are not beginning thinkers.' This statement particularly applies to dyslexic learners.

It is important to be explicit so that students are able to analyse what changes are being made to the sentences as they go along. They should be encouraged to use the correct terms.

Use the opportunity of sentence level work to reinforce word level skills, e.g. when working on adverbs make the link to the consonant suffix 'ly' (the rule is, with consonant suffixes you, 'just add').

The more sophisticated the dyslexic writer becomes, the more they can be encouraged to become analytical and adventurous with their sentences. More information on this approach can be found in the text on 'Kernel sentences' in *Access for All*.

For learners who are working on writing composition at text focus Levels 1 and 2, show them how to experiment with powerful adjectives and adverbs to alter mood and genre. Let them experiment with deleting words to create crisper text whilst still retaining the essential meaning. Show them how to use more complex ways of joining sentences, e.g. 'through', 'since'.

Discuss how the sentence type can be altered in Level 1 work by changing the grammar, choice of words and punctuation.

Sentence	Type of sentence
Don't go there!	Order
Why shouldn't you go there?	Question
I'd rather you didn't go there.	Persuasive
People should not go there.	Statement

Help them to identify when reading how verbs and ancillary verbs (e.g. have, shall, will, was) change when writing in the past, present and future tenses. Ask them to experiment with changing the tense of their own writing and note the impact this has on the prose. Show them how and why main clauses can often stand up on their own as sentences but subordinate clauses cannot. These strategies will support learners working at sentence level across Entry 3 to Level 2.

> 'As he was running to the station   – *subordinate clause*
>   he lost his hat.'   – *main clause*

By linking sentence level work to text level work at Levels 1 and 2 the student will learn how to analyse the structural differences between various types of text, e.g:

- instructional text;
- persuasive text;
- narrative text;
- newspaper reporting;
- formal reports;
- diary form;
- discursive text;
- explanatory text.

He can then experiment with using similar grammatical features to change the style of his own writing.

The spiky profile of the dyslexic learner will almost certainly mean that his sentence level skills outstrip his spelling.

Through work such as that described above we can begin to 'uncork the bottle' so that the sentence level skills can develop despite word level problems.

'When I was young I covered it up by not reading in front of people. If at some time it was unavoidable, I would say I had forgot my glasses. As time went on and if I was given a joke to read I would watch the faces of the people around me to see what their reaction was.'

READING comprehension difficulties can cause many embarrassing moments, as this dyslexic undergraduate describes. The skilled teacher helps the student to develop a smooth interaction between decoding and reading for meaning (bottom up and top down) whilst at the same time continually monitoring the text. The purpose of reading is to comprehend and good comprehenders think as they read, continually checking their understanding.

Research has found that the main causes of poor reading comprehension in dyslexic learners include:

- difficulties in decoding;
- slow reading, which causes a bottleneck for memory;
- difficulty in using syntactical and semantic clues;
- weak working memory where there is not enough memory space to make inferences and to integrate ideas;
- inability to monitor and resolve problems whilst reading.

Poor reading comprehension is associated with poor listening comprehension.

Our aim as teachers is to enable learners to develop the sub-skills of reading such as:

- phonological awareness;
- letter/sound relationships;
- visual memory for letters and words;
- blending;
- splitting words into syllables;

- skimming;
- scanning;
- using semantics;
- prediction;
- vocabulary knowledge;
- interaction with the text;
- inference skills;
- own experience;
- judgements of relevance or bias.

We must use text to integrate these sub-skills so that learners become able to read with fluency and comprehension.

A good diagnostic assessment of reading will inform us which of these sub-skills need most attention. As a general (but not infallible) rule of thumb, phonological dyslexic learners tend to need more work on decoding and word attack skills but they are often quite good at extracting meaning from text, whereas people with visual dyslexia tend to be more reliant on sounding out, and therefore poorer at reading for meaning.

Whilst working with the Core Curriculum we can address the causes of poor reading comprehension in dyslexic learners in a variety of ways.

We have already discussed methods of dealing with decoding problems, which in turn result in slow reading and thus poor comprehension. Work on the word level skills discussed in Chapter 8 will address the first two causes of poor comprehension. Below are some further reading strategies, which will address some of the other causes of poor comprehension.

Inference Skills

Difficulty in using syntactical and semantic clues can be solved by encouraging learners at Level 2 to develop inference skills so that they begin to move from reading *on the line* (literal comprehension) to reading *between the lines* (inferential comprehension).

Consider this paragraph.

'I was brushing the flour off my hands and feeling quite content. From the sitting room I could hear snatches of, "Oh what a good ball", or, "He should have caught that!" and outside the kids were squabbling over which one of them the new batch of chicks would belong to. The kitchen door was open and the smell of hay vied for sweetness with the growing aroma of baking bread. Ian came through to the kitchen for a can of beer. He looked irritable.

"Are they losing?" I enquired unnecessarily. "They're useless", he replied and wandered gloomily back into the sitting room.'

With a passage such as this we can help learners to make inferences by identifying clue words and phrases. For instance, discuss which clue words and phrases give us an idea about:

- where the story takes place;
- what time of year it was;
- what the weather was like.

Questions such as these will encourage a much deeper understanding of the text than the more literal type of question, e.g. *'Why did Ian come into the kitchen?'* Inference skills are required at Levels 1 and 2 text focus.

Signal Words

When reading texts for study, signal words often provide clues as to the author's intentions, e.g:

'important' signal words –	*'a key feature'*
	'a significant factor'
	'a crucial development'
'order' signal words –	*'firstly'*
	'secondly'
	'last'
	'before'
	'after'
'example' signal words –	*'for instance'*
	'an illustration of this'
	'such as'
	'for example'
'summary' signal words –	*'from this we can see'*
	'in conclusion'
	'to summarise'.

Spotting and using signal words helps students to read economically (see Curriculum text focus Rt/E3 & Rt/L1.4).

Key Words

Learners are expected to use keywords to locate information at text level from Entry 3 (see p.72 Rt/E3.7).

Key words, usually nouns and verbs, tend to be the words that generate instant images and so lock ideas into the reader's mind more easily. We can help students to identify the key words initially, by reading a passage to them and asking them to make just one word notes as they listen, not sentences, not phrases, just single words. They then use these individual key words to recall and retell the text after which they turn each key word into a sentence.

The next step would be for the learner to read a text to himself and identify the main points by highlighting the key words.

A development from this stage would be to use colour. Highlight the key words which illustrate the main points in one colour, then use different colours for sub-points, examples, for and against arguments etc. These colour coded key words can then be readily picked out and used for making notes and summaries (word focus).

Dual Code Reading – imaging and language, visualizing and verbalizing

This is an extremely effective technique, which can be taught to dyslexic learners who have difficulty in comprehending and remembering what they have read. It is a multisensory method described by Pat Lindamood (see *Dyslexia Biology Cognition and Intervention,* 1997). The theory is that if dyslexic learners both visualise and verbalise what they have read, they are laying down a more elaborate memory trace for recall. This is helped by using coloured summary squares which act as *'conceptual pegs'.* The dual code technique is most useful as a Level 1/Level 2 skill (see Curriculum p.92 Rt/L2.5). It is carried out as follows.

Word Level

Start by showing the learner a picture, e.g. of a house or a car. Ask him to study it then look away, visualise it, then describe what he 'sees' in his mind's eye using structure words such as colour, size, movement, shape, sound etc. Do the same with a word and ask questions about what he 'sees' in his mind's eye to help him develop the image.

Sentence Level

Progress from this to giving him a short sentence to read and visualise, e.g. *'the man walked up the hill'.* He must then use a small blank card (a summary square) as an 'anchor' for his visualisation. As he puts the card on the table he verbalises what he 'sees'.

'Here I see two men, hot and sweaty, sleeves rolled up
and wearing shorts, stumbling up a lakeland fell.'

Questioning by the teacher develops verbalising skills, the goal being to develop a clear image of the sentence.

Text Level

Now he is ready to progress to paragraphs. It helps at first if the tutor reads the passage, a paragraph at a time (5 paragraphs are usually enough). The student must try to picture in his mind's eye what is going on in the paragraph as it is being read, after which he will pick up a small coloured summary card and say aloud *'Here I see . . .'*, describing the picture of the paragraph he now sees in his mind's eye. He should then place the summary square on the table (nothing is written). The same process takes place with each of the paragraphs.

When the whole text has been read, there should be a vertical row of different coloured cards on the table – one for each paragraph. The student now has to pick up the first summary square and say *'Here I saw . . .'*, describing what he 'saw' in the first paragraph and so on, until he has picked up each card in turn and has described what he 'saw' in each paragraph.

The main idea of the text can be retrieved by 'seeing' what most of the coloured summary squares were depicting and then *'paraphrasing the overall gestalt of the paragraph'* (Lindamood, 1997). Other higher order comprehension skills can be stimulated e.g. inference, conclusion, judgment using questioning by the teacher (see Curriculum p.90 Rt/L2.2).

It is surprising just how much detail can be comprehended, recalled and retained by using this method. It is a very effective method of teaching summary and evaluating skills. This exercise works well with a group of learners, when the tutor reads the text. (Remember that listening comprehension and reading comprehension are associated.) Later on, individual learners can go through the same process, reading the text to themselves. Research has demonstrated significant improvements in comprehension using this method.

There are many other text level strategies which are familiar to basic skills practitioners such as cloze, PQ4R (Preview, Question, Read, Reflect, Recite, Review), DARTs (Directed Activities Related to Text), Tony Buzan's Mind Mapping, and reading alternate paragraphs with a friend, then discussing paragraph by paragraph, what was read. All of these methods can of course be used with dyslexic students.

When using any of these strategies with dyslexic learners it is important to develop students' metacognitive or thinking skills so that they are able to analyse and evaluate their learning. Using a process such as the one described below will help to foster metacognition.

Thinking About Learning (metacognitive skills)

1. *Plan*

    a. The learner should describe out loud what the objective of the task is.

    b. He should plan how he will tackle the task – what steps he will have to take (are there any instructions?)

    c. He will think about what skills he might use.

    d. He will think about what he already knows.

    e. He will collect what materials he needs.

    f. He will decide what methods he will use and in what order to do things.

All of this will be discussed with the teacher.

2. *Do*

The learner will work on the task using the plans he has made, monitoring his performance as he works.

3. *Evaluate*

    a. The learner will think about his methods – were they the best he could have chosen or could they have been improved?

    b. He will check his work looking one at a time for errors, omissions, irrelevancies.

    c. He will check with the original task outline – has he done what he intended?

    d. He can then revise and alter as required.

This process can be used to enhance text level reading or writing. Further ideas on metacognition when reading can be found in the Core Curriculum p.93 Rt/L2.

Modelling

This is a simple but effective way of teaching reading comprehension skills. The teacher reads aloud and 'models' or demonstrates how she comprehends. She should show how she monitors what she is reading, pausing where there is confusion, reading on and back, predicting, clarifying questioning, picking out what is relevant and irrelevant, then summarising. She should show, if and how she might have changed her opinion about the topic after she has read about it, and what new facts she now knows. The student will then do the same and discuss the process with the teacher. This is another form of metacognition. These are some of the skills required at Level 1 reading (text focus).

Visual Aids

People with visual or surface dyslexia often find that it helps to place a sheet of white or coloured paper below the line **below** that which is being read. This blocks out some of the confusion of print but doesn't prevent the follow on from one line to the next. Different coloured acetates, paper or tinted lenses can sometimes help – students and teachers can experiment with these but a specialist optometrist would advise. Antiglare screens or a different coloured background may also reduce the stress of reading from computers. Reading slightly larger print and using a finger or pen to help lead the eyes along the line may also be of benefit.

If teachers are preparing their own text it helps to keep to just one font, create bullet points and headings, and use boxes and plenty of white space. Cream paper is better than white and short paragraphs are better than a dense mass of print. Font size should be big – at least 12 – but not too big, and diagrammatic form is better than linear form. If linear form is used, it is better to 'left justify' only, and have good spaces between paragraphs.

Linking Reading and Writing

Reading as a model for writing

By reading texts written in different genres, such as report, instructional, diary, persuasive, descriptive and so on, learners can begin to analyse and evaluate the key features and how the writer creates these different styles. Practice should be given in categorising the texts of different genres and then looking critically at the contrasting text level, sentence level and word level strategies that the writer uses in each text type. This analytical approach enables the dyslexic adult to unpick texts in a structured way so that he can more easily create his own texts of different genres. A good starting point would be to decide on a topic and write about it in different styles.

The skills required here are at Reading Level 1 (text focus) and Writing Levels1 and 2 (text focus). Throughout the Curriculum, teachers are encouraged to integrate wherever possible, reading and writing skills. In this way, learners come to recognise the relationship between the two and use one to enhance the development of the other.

Writing at Text Level

Writing Frames

One of the most common characteristics of dyslexia is a difficulty with organisational skills. This can be particularly problematic when writing. We can assist dyslexic learners to structure their work by using writing frames which act like a prompt at each stage of composition. Writing frames can be quite basic, such as those described in the Core Curriculum, Wt/E3 p.114-115. Here is an example:

- introduction
- paragraph 1
- paragraph 2
- paragraph 3
- conclusion.

Writing frames can be more elaborate and can suggest opening phrases or sentences for each paragraph or a selection of vocabulary which may be used in each section. Writing frames can act as templates for different styles of writing or even just as prompts for cameo pen pictures. For instance, if a student was asked to write a description of a character, he might categorise his thoughts under what the character looks like, what his personality is, what he likes and dislikes, what his job is, his relationships, his present mood etc. Reading can be used as a model for this type of writing by first reading a good description of a character and analysing the words or phrases the writer uses to describe different aspects of the character. Dickens is a good choice of author for this activity as his descriptions are so rich and detailed. (This work is at word focus Level 1 see Core Curriculum Rw/L1.2 p.84).

Essays and Assignments

If dyslexic students have to write essays or assignments, again one of their main problems is structuring their writing and keeping to the structure. These are primarily Level 2 skills.

The brief guide in Figure 16 may be of use to them.

Figure 16	**Essay Writing Made Easy –** **a five-point plan**

1. Before Writing

Read the question	Make sure you read **all** the words accurately
	Make sure you **understand** all the words
	Write down definitions if necessary
	Make sure you highlight the **key words** so that you're sure you know what is being asked

Gather your material	Get advice on which books/chapters to read
	Write down, using a mind map any ideas you have on the subject
	Use colour to group related ideas
	Read selectively, discarding irrelevancies and make notes while you're reading

2. Still before Writing – Planning

Think about structure; how will you answer the question?

Make an outline plan on one piece of paper, or index cards, or as a mindmap, or on a computer.

Get moving! Move your plan around; cut and paste to find a logical order of thinking.

At this stage	Check against the question
	Check with your course tutor
	Find out about conventions for essay/assignment writing, e.g. length, references, spacing, margins

Plans should show the famous 3 tell 'ems! i.e:

Introduction	– tell 'em how you are going to answer the question
Main body	– tell 'em that you're doing just that; state briefly what each paragraph will be about
	– use different colours for each paragraph
Conclusion	– tell 'em what you've done and state your conclusion.

3. Now you write the first draft

Check the question.

Put the essay title on a card so it can be transferred from page to page or stuck on the front of your computer.

Follow your plan.

For each idea, give relevant examples or accurate referenced quotations.

Keep checking your plan – this is the time when you're most likely to wander off the point!

4. Editing

Read through to get the feel of what you've written, take out irrelevancies and check for omissions.

Check for:
- continuity
- spelling
- grammar and punctuation
- length (10 sheets of A4 is roughly 2500 words, double spaced).

5. Final draft

Re-write

Proofread

Allow thinking time (you may change your mind about some points)

Check the question – have you answered it?

Submit with confidence and breathe a well deserved sigh of relief!

This is Level 2 work (see Core Curriculum Wt/L2.7 p.130)

Using ICT

Information Technology can literally transform a dyslexic adult's life. Advice on appropriate equipment for people in work or looking for work may be available through disablement employment advisers at job centres.

Advice for students in higher education hoping to access ICT equipment via the Disabled Students' Allowance will be available from Access Centres and Disability

Advisers at the appropriate educational institutions. It is possible that the dyslexic student may be given assistance with developing computer skills, or with the purchase or loan of a computer, or both.

Software to support dyslexic students' reading and writing is becoming more sophisticated but is still not perfect.

Texthelp (IANSYST, Lorien) will read out text to the learner. Dragon Dictate is a voice recognition programme which will write what the learner says once it has been trained to his voice.

For further information about these and other programmes see *IT for Dyslexic Adults* (Kaufman, 1998).

Even without these specialised programmes, it is obviously so much easier to shift text about, edit and proofread using a computer. Keyboard skills should be learnt as soon as possible and Touch Type Read & Spell is considered to be useful for this.

Text level skills, like all other literacy skills should be taught to dyslexic learners in a structured explicit multisensory way. For many dyslexic adults the ability to express themselves on paper can be part of the healing process.

These poems were written by a dyslexic adult who is now a talented basic skills tutor and dyslexia specialist. She wrote them when she was just starting out as a volunteer tutor and was acutely aware of her dyslexic difficulties.

Qualified

'You can't be thinking of tutoring,
Not with your history
Forget about the notice
Come on and make me tea.'

'Well I think I've got something to offer'

'You've got a teaching degree?'

'Less of the cheek, mate,
No, I've got empathy.
I know about confusion
Failure isn't news
I could walk in the student's shoes.'

Volunteer Literacy Tutor

Mind growing
No knowing
Who's learning more

Wrong track?
Stand back;
There's an answer for sure.

Fascinating
Answer waiting
Not considered before

Over-load?
– be blowed!
I wouldn't choose another road.

Developing Self-Esteem and a Positive Image

ADULTS who are dyslexic have almost always experienced many years of being told they are lazy, stupid or careless. I recall being in the middle of one assessment of a dyslexic undergraduate when she suddenly said *'I wonder if all dyslexic people were humiliated at school like I was?'*

By the time they reach adulthood there are enormous barriers to break down before they begin to value themselves.

> *'Believe me . . . it has been a curse that has affected every part of my life, everything from the way people see me, to the way in which I see myself. In fact there is nothing about me which has not got a link right back to the simple fact that at times I find it very hard to spell even the smallest words.'*

Self-esteem never develops in a vacuum. It can only start to grow when students discover that they can learn and that the reasons for their difficulties have nothing to do with their intelligence or their worth as people. If we can show them that because of the way their brains are structured, they just learn differently from other people, they will realise that we genuinely value the insights they have to offer and the people they are. In this way we can help them reach their potential. Learning about dyslexia and knowing that we as teachers understand some of its complexities is almost as important to most dyslexic students as improving their literacy skills . . . almost!

The Way Forward

The *Adult Literacy and Numeracy Core Curriculum* with its order and structure presents a unique opportunity for tutors in all basic skills centres to address the challenge of dyslexia in adults. Dyslexic adults do not learn effectively using normal basic skills teaching methods. This handbook can only begin to scratch the surface of this fascinating and rewarding area of work. This is by no means an exhaustive set of suggestions and there will be a great deal more that colleagues can offer to the debate.

Every year more research is being carried out to further our understanding of dyslexia. A better awareness of the condition and more sophisticated technology means that many dyslexic people are now reaching their full potential.

The last word however, must go to a learner.

He is an intelligent man who, when he first came to our Basic Skills Centre, could barely read and write and felt very embarrassed about his difficulties.

One year later, his sense of humour restored, he wrote this true story of how he came to find out about our Centre in the first place. Oh, the pitfalls of being dyslexic . . .

One day I was going to find out
what was wrong with me.
I could not read or write.
So I decided to go to the Citizen's Advice
I went to Redcar and walked around for
a bit.
And then got the courage to go in.
As I went in there was a lad coming
out so I stopped.
The woman said can I help I said I
hope so.
Come in she said sit down.
Have you got an appointment she said

I said I didn't know I needed one.

She said ok you live in Redcar.

No I said

Oh well that's why I have no record
of you. I thought that's odd how could
she have a record of me.

So where do you live. I live in
Grangetown.

Right I will ring the office and tell them
that you are here.

So when did you get out she said.

I said get out of where.

Prison she said you are on parole
aren't you

Hell, I'm only here to see about
my spelling and reading problems.

This is the probation office, she said
The Citizen's Advice office is opposite.

Appendix 1

The LEAP Fast Track Spelling Programme

Spelling Terminology, Logic and Rules

1. Terminology

    1a Consonants, voiced and unvoiced and vowels

    1b Long and short vowel sounds

    1c Syllables, open and closed

    1d Base words

    1e Prefixes and suffixes

    1f Parts of speech (optional)

2. Vowel/consonant patterns

    2a vc, *e.g. hat*

    2b vowel consonant vowel pattern (double vowel power) vcv, *e.g. hate*

3. Syllable division (link to double vowel power logic)

    3a Short vowel pattern – vc/cv, *e.g. rabbit*

    3b Long vowel pattern – v/cv, *e.g. lupin*

    3c Discrimination between long and short vowel pattern

    3d v/v, *e.g. diet*

4. Suffixes (part I)

    4a Consonant suffixes

    4b Vowel suffixes

        (i)   the doubling rule, *e.g. shopping*

        (ii) drop the 'e' rule, *e.g. hoping*

        (iii) ed saying (id), (t) or (d)

5. Useful Rules and Logic

    5a One syllable words with short vowels ending in the sounds (f) (l) or (s) – 'floss' words, *e.g. hiss, pill, cliff*

Appendix 2

Phonological Awareness Exercises

(or linguistic gymnastics!)

Practise some of the exercises each week with your teacher until you feel confident you can hear, discriminate, segment and manipulate sounds in words. (Games can be used to practise any of these skills if you wish.)

1. Count syllables in words – categorise words according to the number of syllables in them.

2. Delete syllables, *e.g. 'painting' without the 'ing', incident without the 'in'.*

3. Blend sounds together into words, *e.g. th – r – u – sh = thrush*

4. Hear the difference between rhyming and non rhyming words, *'pit', 'pat', 'sit'.*

5. Generate rhymes, *e.g. find 6 words that rhyme with 'cat', 'spare' etc.*

6. Identify initial, final and medial phonemes in words: listen and look, *e.g. what's the first sound in ... 'man'? What's the middle sound of the word in this picture? What sound is at the end of 'book'?*

7. Count phonemes in words, e.g. at first by just listening, and later by listening and looking, to identify the corresponding graphemes, *e.g. c – a – t (3), s – t – r – u – ng (5), eigh – t (2).*

8. Delete phonemes from words (just listening).

   (a) Your tutor says a word and then says it again with a sound missing. You have to say which sound is missing.

   (b) Your tutor says a word and tells you which sound she wants you to delete. Then you have to say the word and then repeat it with the given sound missing e.g:

cat without the (c)	=	*at*
ship without the (sh)	=	*ip*
spin without the (sp) sound	=	*in*
spin without the (s) sound	=	*pin*

$$\textit{spin without the (p) sound} \quad = \quad \textit{sin}$$
$$\textit{plate without the (t) sound} \quad = \quad \textit{play}$$
$$\textit{table without the (b) sound} \quad = \quad \textit{tale}$$

(c) Play 'Shrink a Word' – say a word, e.g. 'shrink', say it again, but don't say the (sh) sound, say 'rink', say it again but don't say the (r) sound, say 'ink', say it again but don't say the (k) sound, say 'in', say it again but don't say the (n) sound = (ĭ).

9. Phoneme substitution (just listening).
   - Change one phoneme for another
   - Beginning, medial and end
   - Say a word then say it again with a different phoneme, e.g:

muddle	*(m to c)*	*cuddle*
spot	*(o to a)*	*spat*
tip	*(p to n)*	*tin*
snap	*(n to 1)*	*slap*
mood	*(oo to a)*	*mad, etc.*

10. Say phonemes backwards (just by listening, but look if you need to).
    e.g. $t - e - n \quad > \quad n - e - t$
    $\quad s - t - o - p \quad > \quad p - o - t - s$

11. Spoonerisms, (just by listening – this is the hardest exercise!)
    e.g. *lady / chair* = *chady / lair* etc.

12. Letter/sound correspondence.
    (a) Listen to a piece of text and identify a given phoneme, every time you hear it,
        e.g. *tap on the table every time you hear the long (e) sound.*

    (b) Now read the text and mark all words that have the long (e) phoneme.

    (c) Write the words on cards and categorise them by spelling in columns,
        e.g. *underline the letters that make the phoneme (e); the long (e) sound.*

ee words	ea words	e-e words	ie words	y words	e words
deep	*seat*	*theme*	*piece*	*happy*	*be*
sheep	*meat*	*these*	*field*	*baby*	*me*

    (d) Then read them over, say and picture them, spell them and write them.

(Ideas from *Hatcher's Sound Linkage*)

Appendix 3

MUSP – The Multisensory Spelling Programme for Priority Words

How to learn the words you need in a systematic way, so that they are retained in your long-term memory. In other words, you can always remember how to spell them.

What to do

Week 1

1. Choose a list of between 5 and 15 words that you need to spell; for instance words for work, forms, letters, study etc.

2. Label it list 'A' and date it.

3. Write the words on the left hand side of the page, as whole words in joined up writing.

   On the right hand side of the page, print the word showing the strategy you've chosen.

   (i) Strategies must be multisensory – seeing, hearing and feeling.

   (ii) They must address the bits of the word you are having difficulties with, for instance:

permanent	*perma frost at Nent Head*
necessary	*1 collar and 2 socks (1c and 2s's)*
architect	*arch i tect*
	(visual clue and you say it as it's spelt)
solicitor	*sol ICI tor (note the symmetrical pattern)*
opportunity	*op port unity (split up double consonants auditorily and visually. Find hidden words)*
queue	*q ue ue (say it in rhythm)*
specific	*spec if ic*
always	*al ways one flag.*

   Get the idea?

On a piece of spare paper, fiddle about with a few strategies until you find one that clicks for you.

Important – once you've decided on a strategy, you must stick to it. Your teacher will probably have to suggest strategies to start with, but gradually you'll take over because you know which ones work best for you.

4. Now use the '**Look, Say,** . . . **Cover, Picture it and Say,** . . . **Write, Say,** . . . **Check'** method to practise each word.

   a) **Look** at the word and study the strategy carefully.
   Say the word then **say** the strategy. You must say them out loud.

   b) **Cover** the word and the strategy.
   Say the word, then **say** the strategy, **picture each bit** of the strategy in your mind's eye **as you say it**. At this stage your teacher might ask you to work on the word whilst it's in your mind's eye. For instance you might be asked to identify and spell a middle or end chunk or to spell the word forwards or even backwards by 'reading it off' from your mind's eye image.

   c) **Write** the word as a whole word, in joined up writing but **say** the strategy as you write it – tell your hand what to write.

   d) **Check** letter by letter to see if it's right.

   Don't leave out any stage. Stage 4b is particularly important. Always practise using joined up writing – it develops your motor (muscle) memory.

   During the following week, practise at least a couple of times using the '**Look, Say,** ... **Cover, Picture it and Say,**... **Write, Say,**.... **Check'** method.

Week 2

1. Go over each word and relearn each word and its strategy with your teacher. Always use the above method exactly. Don't be tempted to use short cuts.

2. Let your teacher test you using the following method.
   She says the word, you repeat the word, then say the strategy picturing each bit in your mind's eye **as you say it**. Write the word, saying the strategy as you write it. Don't write it until you can think of the strategy. If you've forgotten, look and say. That's not cheating but learning.

3. Now you must look at your test (without the original) and proofread it for errors like this.

   Say the strategy and look at what you have written. Have you written what the strategy indicates?

4. Only then should you look at the original and mark it.

   During the week – yes, you've guessed it – practise using the above 'Look, Say, . . . Cover, Picture it and Say, . . . Write, Say, . . . Check' method.

   The steps in Week 2 can be repeated in subsequent weeks as often as necessary if you haven't had time to practise at home.

Week 3

Ask your teacher to test you 'cold' without looking first at the list. Use the method described in Week 2, stages 2, 3 and 4. Remember, you must proofread first, then check with original.

During the week practise using the same 'Look, Say, . . . Cover, Picture it and Say, . . . Write, Say, . . . Check' method.

Week 4

a) Your teacher dictates the words you've learnt by putting them into sentences – she says a sentence, you repeat it, write it and proofread it.

b) Start List B – choose new words that have cropped up at work or college and add any words that you're not quite sure of from List A. Use exactly the same system for learning this new list.

MUSP

The Multisensory Spelling Routine
(at a glance)

a) **LOOK** at the word and strategy. **SAY** the word, then **SAY** the strategy.
b) **COVER** the word and the strategy.
   SAY the word then **SAY** the strategy and **PICTURE** each chunk as you say it.
   (Don't forget this stage!)

THEN . . .
c) **SAY** the strategy **AS** you **WRITE** the word.

d) **CHECK**

Jenny Lee

Spelling Safely with Syllables!

This is a way of working out how to spell most 2 syllabled words when adding suffixes.

Vowels are:

a e i o u and sometimes y.

They can be short or long, e.g. căp or cāpe, hŏp or hōpe. 'Y' acts like a vowel if it sounds like a vowel, *e.g. in 'cry' (ī) and 'happy' (ē) or (ĭ), depending on your accent.*

A syllable:

is a **beat** in a word, *e.g. pic nic.*

Syllables can be **open** as in n̄o or b̄e.
Here the vowel is long because there is no consonant wall blocking it.

Or they can be **closed** as in nŏt and bĕt.
Here we have a consonant wall blocking in the vowel and keeping it short. If we turn *'not'* into *'note'* we need **double vowel power.**

Double vowel power logic goes like this: if there is only 1 consonant wall, the extra vowel 'e' can break down that wall and turn the short (ŏ) into a long (ō).

Two syllabled words

In words of two syllables, if you treat each syllable independently, you can easily work out how to spell and read them.

To split words logically into syllables, mark the vowel with a 'v' for vowel and mark the consonants **between** the vowels with a 'c' for consonant.

If there are 2 consonants, you always divide **between** the consonants as in:

VC/CV
rab/bit.

Here, the first syllable is closed and therefore has a short vowel sound – răb.
If there is only 1 consonant between the vowels, you usually divide before the consonant like this:

V/CV
bi/ped.

The first syllable is open: 'bī', therefore it has a **long** vowel sound.

Regrettably, there are some exceptions *e.g.* 'rŏbin', but these tend to be common words, which are either already known or can be learnt as exceptions.

(Curriculum reference Ww/E3.2 p.118.)

Adding suffixes

A suffix is a letter, or group of letters added to a baseword. There are **vowel** suffixes that start with a vowel, *e.g.* 'ing', 'ed', 'y', 'able' or **consonant** suffixes that start with a consonant, e.g. 'ly', 'ness', 'ful', 'ment'. The spelling of suffixes never changes – DO NOT DISTURB a suffix!

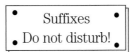

Vowel suffixes

The double vowel power logic we've learnt becomes really useful when adding vowel suffixes and there are virtually no exceptions here.

The word *hop* is a closed syllable and therefore has a short vowel sound. What happens when we add *ing*?

We need to keep the first vowel short when we add *ing*, so we must prevent double vowel power by adding an extra consonant wall.

VC/CV

hŏp + p + ing = hop/ping (the first syllable is closed so the vowel is short).

For curriculum reference see Ww/L1, spelling and word structure p.125.

Try this one: māke (here the 'e' is doing its double vowel power act, lengthening the 'a') + *ing*.

We have now got a vowel suffix which will perform the double vowel power function instead of the 'e'. (You can't have triple vowel power.)

V/CV

Therefore: māke + ing = ma/king (the first syllable is open, so the vowel is long).

Try some more: mate + ing   =   mat + ing

                          rate + ing   =   rat + ing

You will need lots of practice, and to begin with you'll need to work out the logic every time. Later you will be able to spot syllable patterns when reading and hear whether to double or drop when adding suffixes for spelling.

Consonant suffixes

Adding consonant suffixes is even easier.
Remember consonant suffixes start with a consonant, *e.g.* 'ly', 'ty', 'ful', 'ment', 'ness', 'less'. The rule here is this:

> when adding a **consonant** suffix, you **leave** the **base word alone.**
> (There is only one exception and that's when the base word ends in 'y'.)

So if you know how to spell the base word and you know how to spell the suffix, you can't go wrong, e.g:

love + ly = lovely	*faith + ful + ly = faithfully*
hope + ful = hopeful	*sincere + ly = sincerely.*

For curriculum reference see Ww/E3, spelling and word structure p.119.

Suffixing logic continued . . . the soft c and g

Listen to these words:

goat, gash, grip	*here we have a hard (g) sound*
gentle, gist, gypsy	*here we have a soft (j) sound*
cat, cot, cut	*here we have a hard (k) sound*
centre, city, cycle	*here we have a soft (s) sound.*

Can you spot the rule?
If a 'c' or a 'g' are followed by an 'e', 'i' or 'y' they sound soft (s) or (j).
Knowing this helps when adding suffixes. If the end of the word needs to have a soft (j) or (s) sound, then it must be followed by an 'e', 'i' or 'y'.

Watch:

notice + ing = noticing (you can drop the 'e' because the vowel suffix begins with 'i');

notice + able = noticeable (you must keep the 'e' to keep the soft (s) sound because 'able' doesn't start with 'e' 'i' or 'y';

manage + ing = managing (you can drop the 'e' because the vowel suffix starts with an 'i');

manage + ment = management (it's a consonant suffix, so you would just add it in any case);

Manage + able = manageable (the 'e' must stay because the vowel suffix does not begin with an 'e', 'i', or 'y'.

More logic with soft 'c' and 'g'. Can you describe the 2 jobs of the 'e' in the word *cage?*

It is doing its double vowel power act and lengthening the 'a'. It is also softening the 'g'.

In badge we only need the 'e' to soften the 'g' so we must have an extra consonant wall; in this case it's always a 'd'.

If you are unsure whether you need the 'd' just listen to the vowel sound – if it is long you do not need the wall, if it is short you do.

$$rage_{\text{VCV}} \qquad\qquad hedge_{\text{VCCV}}$$

Now add a suffix: rage + ing = raging, hedge + ing = hedging

Try these:

cadge + er = ... cage +ing = ...

More Double Vowel Power (only just!)

Many words end in what is known as a regular final syllable, *e.g. dle, cle, tle, ple, ble, gle.*

For the purposes of our logic, 'le' can be thought of as a vowel unit, so if the word has a short vowel sound, you need 2 consonant walls before the vowel unit.

e.g: *apple   kettle*

If there is a long vowel sound in the word, *eg: rifle, table, bugle,* there is only one consonant wall before the vowel unit.

For Curriculum reference see Ww/L1, spelling and word structure p.125.

Now that you have seen the logic you will need to spend time working on each part of Spelling Safely with Syllables.

Do plenty of exercises where you STOP AND THINK before writing the word so that you have to work out the logic. Then use the words in text, but to begin with, always STOP AND THINK until you begin to automatically recognise the patterns when reading, and they are 'in your hand' when spelling.

References

Akshoomoff & Courchesne, (1992) *A New role for the Cerebellum in Cognitive Operations*, Behavioural Neuroscience Vol 106, No 5, 731-738.

Alexandre P., *Touch Type Read and Spell Computer Course.*

Bramley W., *Literacy for Study and Work,* The Dyslexia Institute.

DfES, (2000) *Freedom to Learn – Basic Skills for Learners with Learning Difficulties and/or Disabilities,* the report of the working group looking into the basic skills needed for adults with learning difficulties and disabilities.

DfES, (2002) *Access for All.*

Fawcett A.J. & Nicolson R.I., *Dyslexia Adult Screening Test,* London: The Psychological Corporation.

Fawcett A.J., & Nicolson R.I., (1994) *Dyslexiain Children, Multidisciplinary Perspectives*, London: Harvester Wheatsheaf.

Fawcett A.J., & Nicolson R.I., (1999) *Dyslexia: The Role of the Cerebellum,* Dyslexia and International Research and Practice, Vol 5, 155-177.

Fawcett A.J., ed (2001) *Dyslexia Theory & Good Practice,* London: Whurr Publishers Ltd.

Frith U., (1997) In Hulme. C. & Snowling M., (1997) *Dyslexia, Biology Cognition and Intervention*, London: Whurr Publishers Ltd.

Hatcher, P. J., (1994) *Sound Linkage,* London: Whurr.

Hornsby B. & Shear F., (1974) *Alpha to Omega,* Heinemann.

Hulme C. & Snowling M., (1997) *Dyslexia, Biology Cognition and Intervention*, London: Whurr Publishers Ltd.

Klein C., (1993) *Diagnosing Dyslexia,* London: ALSBU (now The Basic Skills Agency).

Kaufman C., (1998) *IT for Dyslexic Adults,* British Dyslexia Association, 98 London Road, Reading, RGI 5AU.

Leiner H.C., Leiner H.L. & Dow R.S., (1993) *Cognitive & Language Functions of the Human Cerrebellum,* Trends in Neuroscience, 16, 444-447.

Livingstone M., Rosen, G. D., Drislane F. & Galaburda A., (1991) *Physiological Evidence For A Magnocellular Defect In Developmental Dyslexia*, Proceedings of the National Academy of Sciences, 88, 7943-7947.

Lovegrove W.J., Garzia R.P. & Nicholson S.B., (1990) *Experimental Evidence of a Transient System Deficit in Reading Disability*, Journal of the American Optometric Association, 61, 137-146.

McLoughlin, Fitzgibbon & Young, (1994) *Adult Dyslexia Assessment, Counselling & Training*, London: Whurr Publishing Ltd.

Paulesu E., Frith U., Snowling M., Gallagher A., Morton J., Frackowiak R., Frith C., (1996) *Is Developmental Dyslexia a Disconnection Syndrome? Evidence from PET Scanning*, Brain, 119, 143-157.

Pietrowski J. & Reason R., (in press) *The National Literacy Strategy & Dyslexia.*, Support for Learning 15, 1.

Singleton, C. H. (Chair), (1999) *Dyslexia in Higher Education: Policy Provision and Practice. The Report of the National Working Party on Dyslexia in Higher Education*, Hull: University of Hull.

Rack J., (1995) *Phonological Processing & Developmental Dyslexia*, Journal of Research into Reading, Vol 18, 132-138.

Townend J. & Turner M. ed, (2000) *Dyslexia in Practice – A Guide for Teachers*, Plenum Publishing Corporation Ltd/Kluwer Academic.

Vinegrad, *Adult Dyslexia Checklist*, London: Adult Dyslexia Organisation.

Walker J., Brooks L., (1993) *The Dyslexia Institute Literacy Programme (DILP)*, London: James & James Ltd.

Wilkinson G., WRAT, (1993) *Wide Range Achievement Test*, Wide Range Inc., Wilkington, Delaware USA.

Wood E., (1982) *Exercise Your Spelling*, Sevenoaks: Hodder & Stoughton

Yap R.L. & van der Leij A., (1994) *Automaticity Deficits in Word Reading*, in Fawcett and Nicholson ed. *Dyslexia in Children – Multidisciplinary Perspectives*, Chapter 3.